MW00698186

Sunshine After the Storm:

A Survival Guide for the Grieving Mother

Edited by: Alexa Bigwarfe

A collection written for grieving mothers by mothers who have found their way after the death of a baby or child

Library of Congress Control Number 2013
All rights reserved.
ISBN-10:
0989934713
ISBN-13:
978-0-9899347-1-8
Edited by Alexa Bigwarfe& Kelly McGough
Cover Design by CsizMEDIA

Dedication

To Aunt Beth, Beth K., Cortlin, Sami, Waneta, Stacy, ReNee, Renee, Kelly, Carrie, Susan B., Jodi, Charlotte, Meg C., Kimberly, Tracy, Jennifer, Andrea, Karen, Ruth, & all of the lovely contributors in this book. I hate that we have this in common, but I am thankful for the love and support you provide. To my sweet Kathryn…your two days on earth were so cherished. I miss you. Thank you for making me a better person. Thank you Jeff for encouraging me. Braedan, Ella, and Charis, I love you. — Alexa Bigwarfe

Dedicated to my wonderful husband, family, and friends, in loving memory of our Neverborns, Jesse (02.11.12) and Sam (09.03.13). And to every woman who feels isolated by her loss: From my heart to yours, I promise you, you're not alone. — Lizzi Rogers

To Leo, who held me up and kept me laughing even when there wasn't much to laugh about, and Rocco, who will always live on in my heart. — AnnMarie Gubenko

I would like to thank the five angels who came before my three sweet children. They have made me a much better, more appreciative mother. And to my husband, Joe Radigan, who has been by my side through all the twists and turns of our parenting journey.
- Kathy Radigan

I would like to thank those good folks in my life most responsible for making me a mom: my loving and supportive husband, Jeremy; my mom, the original Donna, who taught me so much with her own mothering, but who never lived long enough to see me mother; and my children, those who give me purpose and joy — the beautiful Donna, the sweet Jay, and the gifted Adler. — Sheila Quirke

To Susan Killeen, whom God used at just the right time.
— Sandi Haustein

I dedicate my writing to my beautiful family: David, who shines the light when I am in dark places; Lakin and Addah, who make me smile when skies are gray; and sweet Clara, who captured my heart without ever taking a breath. They are my inspiration and my reason for being.
— Heather Webb

To my angel babies Leo, Mary, Tucker, Lily, and Nina, thank you for bringing me closer to myself, deeper into the fullness of life. Carrying each of you was a gift. Always and forever, Mom, xoxo.
— Suzanne M. Tucker

To my family: Tim, Margaret, and Jack. Jack, we love you. We miss you. We'll never forget you.
— Anna Whiston-Donaldson

Gone but never forgotten. We love you, Jason!
— Marcia Kester Doyle

To all my children, I exist because of you. — Amy Hillis

To my husband Eric, who has stood beside me for better or for worse; to Lydia and Caleb, my miracles on Earth; and to Naomi, Kyria, and Jordan, my little ones in heaven. I love each one of you, more than my heart can tell.
— Kristi Bothur

I would like to dedicate my contribution in this book to all of the mothers and fathers who parent children who are no longer among the living: may this book help spread love, light, peace and hope during the dark days. — Regina Petsch

Dedicated to my beautiful daughters, Ladybug, Sunshine, Daisy, and my precious Rainbow. You all bring light into my life, each in your own way. I love you. -Tova Gold

"To Hadley, who left us with the most heartbreakingly beautiful understanding of what life really is." - Jessica Watson

Finally, this book is dedicated not only to all of the mothers and fathers who have suffered through the death of a child or infertility, but to all of the amazing people who support us in our struggles. Thank you to everyone who played a part in each of us finding our sunshine after the storm.

Acknowledgments

This book would not be possible without the efforts of many people. Thank you first and foremost to all of the contributors, for pouring their hearts out and reliving difficult moments in the hopes of helping someone else.

Thank you to Crystal Ponti of *Blue Lobster Book Co.* for walking me through this process and sharing so much information.

Sherokee Ilse, Jessica Zucker, and Sean Hanish – I appreciate your input and time more than you can imagine. Thank you all so much for all that you do for the community of grieving parents.

Kelly McGough– fantastic job editing and helping me through this immense project.

Brooke Warner – thank you for being such a great writing coach and source of information.

Jeff – you've been my biggest cheerleader. Thank you for helping me follow this path. I love you.

Contents

Survival Tip #13 Recognize that men grieve differently, but they still grieve.

Chapter Eight: There Is Not Always a Reason Why...**215**
Survival Tip #14 Don't drive yourself crazy, trying to find a "reason," because some things can never be understood.

Survival Tip #15 If you have to make a choice that sucks, know that just because you have to make it, it does not mean you loved your baby less or suffered any less.

Chapter Nine: Grieving the Death of a Multiple..**235**
Survival Tip #16 You are allowed to grieve the loss of a baby, even if you take another baby home.

Chapter Ten: It Gets Better... Easier... Eventually..................................**245**

Survival Tip #17 Open yourself up to allowing time to heal you; it does get easier.

Survival Tip #18 Find a way to handle your grief.

Survival Tip #19 "Go to the joy." Choose life.

Survival Tip #20 Keep the memories alive and honor your child.

Survival Tip #21 Let happiness find you again.

Survival Tip #22 Control your own happiness.

Chapter 11: The Ever After—Helping Others through Our Loss...**297**

Survival Tip #23 Help others through this miserable journey; you will find joy and peace.

Conclusion - You Are Not Alone

Extras

Grief Checklist

My Grief To-Do List

Grief Resources

Contributor Bios

Foreword

If you have had a baby die, you **KNOW**. You *know* that life changes and you will never return to your "old self." You *know* that people treat you differently yet want you to be the same person you were. The one they knew so it was easier. Easier to talk with you and be with you and look forward to a predictable future. But there is nothing predictable or planned about the journey that is called grief after the death of a child.

You *know* that time does not make this better by itself, that grieving is hard work and there is no exact prescription, and that while others can be there some of the time, you are there all of the time.

And if you are someone who loves a grieving mother or father, you **KNOW**. You *know* that words don't come easy and anything you try to say can come out wrong. You *know* that you feel inadequate and confused. What do they need? How you do you help? When do you come? When do you go? Why can't you take their pain away, and should you try? With more questions, you realize you don't know anything (or much) about how to be a good support to a mother after her child dies.

These things aren't typically taught. They are learned. The hard way!

When one's child dies too soon (it's always too soon), the fallout is like the atom bomb. Unbelievable and without words to describe what just happened and what to do next. The devastation is vast and consuming. You love them so much, and you never,

never could imagine burying your child. When it happens to you, indeed, you *know* what it feels like to have leprosy, the plague, tuberculosis, and AIDS all at once. You are overwhelmed with pain and emotions, and too many people won't come near; but if they do, they often don't know what to say or do.

Then there can be the struggles of understanding and support that may occur between spouses or within your faith community, at work, and even in your family. Alone. Lonely. Isolated. Crazy. Confused. Buried in deep sand or muck. Struggling to breathe, to sleep, to hear, to do, to live.

It doesn't matter if that baby is a tiny light blinking on the ultrasound screen who doesn't get past 7 weeks. It doesn't matter if that child died somewhere during pregnancy before 40 weeks. It doesn't matter if this is a baby who is going to die or be severely challenged, or a termination of a loved baby has occurred in order to spare the child and family pain and heartache. And it doesn't matter if the baby lived for hours, days, weeks, or years and then died.

Yes, having a child die, no matter when and no matter how, seems hardly survivable.

Yet that is what a mother must do. Find ways to survive. One minute, one day at a time.

Sunshine After the Storm is an amazing answer to aide in the struggle to survive. With heartfelt stories on many of the various topics and issues mothers face, you will feel surrounded by others who "get it."

While you may or may not find every concept, every story, or every style of grief language fits for you, you will definitely find affirmation and support, no matter *your* story.

Clearly, you are not alone.

Every story is valid, real, and personal. But not so personal that you won't sigh, shake your head with understanding, or touch your heart and say, "I am not the only one." Maybe you will also say, "I feel the Sisterhood of Love...women who offer me hope, encouragement, and understanding." It would be wonderful if you can also say, "If they survived, and even thrived after such a devastating loss, maybe I can, too."

The entire book is full of honest, raw stores of love and loss. It can be oh so helpful to mothers and fathers who have had a child die.

Whether through a miscarriage, stillbirth, neonatal death, or later loss...clearly these children matter to their families.

Story after story express the love and the dreams mothers have for their children and their lives. And they also tell of the depth of despair after their child's death along with how they coped and came to a place where they could reach out to help others. A miracle, really.

From getting out of bed and beginning to function again when the center of one's universe has died too soon. Then to have enough courage and strength to dare to share one's inner thoughts and even advice to others...well, that is also a miracle. It just goes to show the power of a mother's love and concern for other mothers who find themselves in the dank puddle of grief and loss.

You will read of wallowing, complaining, and mountains of frustration and pain. And you will read of courageous choices of joy and pride at being a mother and being a survivor.

For example, Stephanie writes, "I'd like to say that I found a place within me during those blackest of months to gain the perspective that someday everything would be okay. But the truth is, I merely survived it. The perspective came later, when I no longer realized I was looking for it. It takes time to get through that tunnel. Don't rush yourself; allow yourself to be right where you are, honor the full spectrum of your feelings, and surround yourself only with those who build you up and protect you. Build yourself a cocoon for as long as you like, and be assured, when it is time to come out of it, you will emerge."

This type of message is found throughout this book. The raw realities of life after loss are shared, yet positive affirmations and perspectives of honoring and remembering also abound. The ups and downs of suffering and growth make this journal-like compilation a must-read for mothers who have gone home to sad houses and fruitless beds.

Dive in.

To any page, any story.

You'll find what you need when you need it. Trust that. These mothers are prepared to meet you where you are. They have learned and grown and know it is now your turn. Your time.

Because when you love someone that much, of course it will hurt even more. A tribute, really, to the value of their lives. Parents now **know** what being a parent means. It isn't easy and there are no guarantees, but through it all, love is the deepest. Most abiding emotion. The one that eventually will carry you through to the other side.

That and finding your Sisterhood.

Sherokee Ilse
International Bereavement Educator/Speaker
Author, *Empty Arms*
(952) 476-1303
www.BabiesRemembered.org
www.LossDoulasInternational.com

Sherokee Ilse is a bereaved mother who became a pioneer in the area of infant loss. She is an international expert, consultant, author, and most importantly a parent's advocate. As an author of 17 books and booklets on baby loss and death and dying, she has spoken at thousands of meetings, support groups, conferences, inservices, and multiple day seminars. A guest of many local, regional, and national television shows including Oprah and Donahue, she has been consulted by the media and institutions who support families extensively over the 32 years of her passionate work in this field.

Ms. Ilse has consulted with hospitals to improve their programs and works with families who need support and assistance in working with their hospitals, funeral homes, vital statistics, and other systems. She has co-founded a new Parent Advocate Certification Program - **Loss Doulas International**, which empowers parents to gain a bit of control and make the best decisions possible at the time of their loss and in the days that follow. The intention is to help them minimize regrets and maximum memories while honoring their child's sacred life.

If you need help, wish to network with others, or seek something not easily found on our website, contact Sherokee at: **sherokeeilse@yahoo.com**

Introduction

The idea for this book came about at the memorial service for a stillborn baby. My friend was over 37 weeks pregnant with her baby girl when a knot in her umbilical cord took her from her mommy and daddy too soon. The night of the service, as I stood in the atrium of the church, talking with my friend Kelly, another "loss mom" and contributor to this book, we discussed amongst ourselves how great it would be if we could just impart to our dear friend all of the knowledge that we have gained since our losses. We wanted to make it all instantly better for her, and provide her everything she needed to survive this terrible ordeal. Even though we knew this was a journey she would have to endure on her own, we wanted to make sure she knew she didn't have to do it alone.

I told Kelly I'd been writing tips on my blog on how to help a grieving mother survive, but perhaps I should consider writing some tips to actually help the grieving *mother*. And the seed was planted.

The concept began as a project to provide encouragement and began to evolve into the "survival guide" concept. We decided to tell more than just our stories of loss, but how the losses changed and transformed us, in addition to all of the things we have learned along the way that have helped or hindered us in our journey.

We are not doctors, psychologists, or trained counselors. We are, however, experienced grieving mothers. And we hope to bring you comfort and encouragement by sharing our understanding and advice.

This book is not designed exclusively for pregnancy and infant loss. We also share the stories of mothers whose older children died too soon, and how their worlds have been rocked by loss.

Even if your baby was an adult when he or she died, they were still, and will always be, your baby.

A few months after my daughter Kathryn died, a very good friend's sister died of ovarian cancer. Jennifer had been fighting for seven years on and off. Her funeral was in March 2012. I had just brought my surviving twin home after three months in the Neonatal Intensive Care Unit (NICU), and I was still numb with pain from the loss of my other baby. I was absolutely struck by the grace of Jennifer's mother. She stood in the receiving line for all those who came to grieve the loss of *her daughter*. She was beautiful and poised, wearing a pair of sassy sandals that showcased her bright teal toenails.

Teal, the color of support for ovarian cancer.

Teal, the color of *hope* for this mother.

Despite the fact that her own baby girl had just passed away, at only thirty-eight years old, Linda comforted *me* for my loss when I reached her in the receiving line. We shared a very knowing hug — the hug that only mothers who have experienced the loss of their child can share.

Five short months later, Linda passed away unexpectedly herself. Her death was shocking and an unfair tragedy for my friend's family. I believe she died quite literally of a broken heart and from the stress of years of caring for her ailing daughter. I often picture Jennifer, who never had a chance to have babies of her own, holding my Kathryn in her arms, with Linda lovingly at her side.

Having a child die, regardless of age, is devastating. Your heart may be shattered in a million pieces. I watched my grandmother suffer after the loss of her only daughter. My aunt died of ovarian cancer when I was two years old. I do not remember her, but I know how much her loss impacted my grandmother. Of course my grandfather also grieved profoundly, but in a much less open manner. I do not believe my grandmother's broken heart ever completely healed. Recently my father gave me my grandmother's poem journal. She loved to write and to collect inspirational quotes and poems. The most encouraging is "A Child of Mine" by Edgar Albert Guest, which was later reprinted for a female child and describes a conversation from God to the mother, telling her that the child was perhaps not with her for long, but she was chosen especially to mother that child. It is a beautiful and hopeful piece. You can find this poem easily online.

I know that my grandmother suffered greatly, and yet she wrote with such hope and faith in her journal.

Such is the purpose of this book.

Hope.

Encouragement.

Sisterhood.

Understanding.

Our stories range from struggles with infertility, multiple losses, early pregnancy losses, stillborn babies, and infant loss, to the loss of children. We pour our hearts out in this book about the impact of those losses on our lives, the range of emotions we experienced, the impact of words and actions of others on our grieving process, and our feelings on how faith did or did not impact us through this journey. We are here for you. A sisterhood of love.

Isolation is a common theme reiterated throughout this book. You will find many ideas repeated over and over throughout the book. This is because no matter how different our actual experience was, we have all experienced many of the same emotions: isolation, shame for our emotions, guilt, awkwardness, anger, a feeling of insignificance, a sense of failure, and so forth. Many of the contributors state that they had the impression after their loss that there was no one who understood their pain.

Until they came across another grieving mother.

When another mother who has suffered this same loss offers words of encouragement, the words carry a different weight entirely. It is almost as if there is an invisible thread that connects grieving mothers. In fact, many of the women in this book became "insta-friends" of mine solely because of the bond that we share from our losses. Our connections have only grown stronger, particularly as we planned how to best serve other grieving mothers.

We have all come to the same overall conclusion. Our lives changed because of our loss. We are different. And we are surrounded by an army of mothers who know and understand these emotions and welcome us with open arms.

Into the club you never wanted to join, but paid the highest dues.

It's also a club made up of the most genuine and supportive members you will ever know. One of the neatest things about writing this book was the interaction with all of these contributors in our secret Facebook group. Not only did we carefully and thoughtfully decide what and whom to include in this book, we shared personal stories and comforted each other. We *encouraged* each other. We hope to duplicate this effort as you read this book. And if you want to interact, we invite you to join our Facebook page at http://www.facebook.com/SunshineAftertheStorm

Grief is messy, grief is individual, and grief cannot be put on a timetable or expected to follow any "rules." Although no one can magically get you beyond your grief and you do have to find your way through this muck, you do not have to do it on your own. Knowing that circumstances vary so greatly and not all of these tips will be applicable to every person, you can read this book straight through, or you can choose to read the sections that you feel are most applicable. Most of these stories could be included under multiple tips, but I tried to find the stories that fit best to illustrate the points we are trying to make.

Although we know that fathers grieve too, this book is written primarily *for* mothers because it is written primarily *by* mothers. Fathers often grieve in a more private way than mothers. However, we have included a special chapter dedicated just to the grieving father, with input from four fathers who have experienced the death of a baby. Additionally, you will find some resources in the Grief Resources section for fathers.

Finally, this book can be shared with friends and family to perhaps help give them a little insight into the window to your soul.

Wishing you peace,

Alexa Bigwarfe
No Holding Back

"Our shared circumstances brought us closer together, and I found that she was the only person I wanted to talk to during those challenging weeks.

—Stephanie S.

Chapter 1: The Ties that Bind Us

This sucks. It is ugly. It is raw. There is just no nice way to describe it. The worst thing you can ever imagine happening to you has just happened.

Now what?

I wish that I could offer you a magic solution to make it all better instantly.

I wish I could take away that pain and hurt and just transport you to a time when it does not hurt as badly.

But I cannot. It is a road that you will have to travel and a time that you will have to trudge through before you are able to dig yourself out of this pit.

However, what I can do, and what *we* can do as fellow grieving mothers, is wrap our arms around you and let you know that you are not alone. We can share our stories with you, we can assure you that time will help you get beyond this initial pain, and we can bring our shovels to help dig you out of the pit.

Repeat after me: "I am not alone."

My first experience with infant loss was through the wife of a friend. She had a full-term baby die when the cord wrapped around the baby girl's neck. Although I did not have children of my own then, I was so saddened for their loss. My husband and I attended the funeral, and the sight of that tiny casket is forever burned in my brain. (That memory played a large role in my decision to cremate my own daughter. I could not bear the thought of another tiny casket.) I tried to be strong for my friend, but I sobbed as I hugged her. She was stone, but I was a mess. And seven years later, I found myself in her shoes, stunned and comforting other people who did not know what to say or do for me.

Immediately following the loss of my two-day-old infant, I felt terribly alone. I believed not a soul in the world could possibly understand the range of emotions that I felt, including sadness, anger, guilt, loneliness, fatigue, and even relief (which just increased the guilt!). I found it difficult to communicate my emotions with family and friends. I was so angry that their lives seemed untouched by this event that stopped mine in its tracks. (I know this is not true. They grieved as well, but often were at a loss for how to express their feelings.)

But then something incredible began to happen. I received cards and letters from other women who had lost a baby. Some had never shared their story with anyone before. And I felt their arms wrap around me in a way that no one else in my inner circle could do, no matter how much they loved me.

It took eight months before I sought out a grief support group. I wish I had gone earlier. Being in the presence of women who completely understood my emotions, and who didn't find it awkward or strange to listen to me talk about my experience, feelings, and my daughter, was amazingly cathartic. It warmed my heart to say her name, Kathryn, and share her with women who really wanted to listen.

I also found that the more I was willing to share my story, the more women admitted to me that they had also experienced a loss. Even as long as forty years after the loss of their baby, these women still shed tears as they talked about their baby. I realized that this is a pain that, while it will ease, will never go away.

On average, the worst of the grieving period is for about the first 18–24 months. But that does not mean it just ends after that time frame. Throughout this book, we hope to show you that there are many ways to grieve. Some ways are better than others. There is no timeline, and even if you think you are okay, there may be days that still come at you with a tremendous force. This is normal. And nothing is normal. You will learn to live in what many of us call "the new normal."

For some reason, our society seems to close our eyes to the pain, suffering, and intense loss felt by the mothers who have babies earlier in the pregnancy. Interestingly, in my support group I have found that it is often those mothers who feel the most intense grief. There is evidence from at least one study that these mothers grieve because they view this as a "baby," not just an event. I've listened to mother after mother talk about how they felt like they were not allowed to grieve their early pregnancy loss. And if they were grieving, they felt that those around them expected them to move on quickly. Or worse, they never told anyone about their loss because they had already been made to feel that at that time frame, *the baby did not matter.* Everyone experiences the death of loved ones, but there is something different when it is a child who dies. Whether that child was as small as a tiny grain of sand in the early stages of formation, or forty-two years old when they passed on, there is nothing quite like a mother's grief.

We are here to tell you that even if you were pregnant for only a few short weeks, it is okay for you to grieve that loss. You had a baby who died too soon. And you will always wonder what your life could have or would have been like with that child in your life.

You may feel more alone than you ever have, and perhaps you do not have any friends or immediate family who have gone through this experience, but you now have a new community to lean on.

You are not alone. We are here.
Xoxo,
Alexa B.

Kathryn and Charis

By Alexa Bigwarfe

If the babies can just be born alive, I know they will make it!

This is the thought that kept me going day after day as I lay in an uncomfortable hospital bed, waiting to find out if the death sentence my babies had been given would come to fruition, or if a miracle might happen.

I was pregnant with identical twin girls. Upon learning about the twins, I had no idea how high risk identical twins were. When identical twins share a placenta, there is a 20 percent risk that they will develop Twin to Twin Transfusion Syndrome (TTTS). When my doctor mentioned the possibility, she said it so nonchalantly, assuring me that if this ever developed, there were things that could be done to fix it. So for me, it was not a concern.

Until the 20-week anatomy scan, when we learned that Baby A had fluid building up in her abdomen and around her heart, and Baby B was 50 percent too small.

With TTTS, the babies do not share the placenta equally. One baby passes extra fluids to the other, leaving it without enough fluids and overloading the other twin. Our Baby A was being overwhelmed by excess fluids, and it would kill her if something was not done.

We went through three hospitalizations and multiple procedures to try to save the babies, but Baby A, later named Kathryn, continued to worsen, and Baby B was growing too slowly. But I held on to hope. I prayed for a miracle. As Kathryn's condition deteriorated, I felt myself losing hope, and losing faith.

We finally, amazingly made it to 28 weeks' gestation, and Baby B finally surpassed 500 grams.

I held on to that one thought.

If the babies can just survive until they are born, they will make it!

Lying in a hospital bed on bed rest for weeks, waiting to learn our fate, I began to believe in modern medicine more than I believed in miracles.

I was failed by both.

Our daughters were both born alive. I went into labor at 30 weeks and 5 days. Charis was actually born first, now becoming Baby A. My heart rejoiced as I heard the tiny squeaks of her cry. We did not expect to hear either baby cry. She was breathing on her own, even at only 1 pound 10 ounces. I felt intense relief.

Then came Kathryn. There was no sound. She was 4 pounds 6 ounces, largely due to fluid. Her belly was distended terribly from the excess fluid, and her heart was failing. She was not breathing and had to be resuscitated and intubated. But she was alive. They could save her.

The babies were rushed off to the NICU. My husband followed.

Over the next two days, we learned the limits of modern medicine.

The damage caused to Kathryn by the continued excessive fluid in her system was just too much. Her heart failed her, and her lungs were too small to support her body. The doctors exhausted all avenues they knew to try to save her.

After fifty-two hours, it was time to say good-bye. I held that beautiful baby girl in my arms and felt my heart break into a million pieces.

In some ways, I consider myself lucky.

I had ten weeks to prepare myself for the death of one or both of my babies.

I had another baby who was still alive, although not out of the woods yet, but not facing the immense complications her sister battled.

Both of my babies were born alive, so the world acknowledged both of them as "real."

But in that moment, as they handed Kathryn to me to hold and she took her last struggled breaths, none of that mattered to me.

The pain ripped my whole being to shreds. In that moment, the only thing I knew was that the child that I carried, that I dreamed of, that I *loved intensely,* was leaving me forever.

And my world would never be the same.

That moment broke something inside of me. There is the "Alexa, before losing Kathryn" and the "Alexa, post-losing Kathryn," and they are different people. But truthfully, I like the person that I have become since losing my baby. I am less concerned about trivial crap. I could care less about silly drama because I know what real pain and suffering is. I am more open to trying things and living life, taking hold of my dreams and moving forward. I treasure my living children more than I ever thought possible. I have an immense compassion, particularly for grieving mothers, but for all people who struggle in this world.

This change did not happen overnight, and it did not happen on my own. I am a work in progress. I am only twenty-one months out from my loss, but I am healing. My "Life After Loss" support group and my friends (many of them new friends) who have experienced the loss of a baby or child, or went through the hellish nightmare of TTTS, like Tova, Wendy, Christina, and Megan (contributors to this book), are helping me day by day.

I became very closely connected to a sweet woman named Jennifer, who lives in Kentucky and I've never had the pleasure of meeting in real life. One night we happened to be on the Facebook page for TTTS Survivors Support. (There are few members on the page who have only a single survivor, a connection Jennifer and I also share.) It was late, and we were both in a particularly silly mood, I suppose. She lost her precious son, Bryce, and is raising her surviving twin, Chayce. We started joking about Bryce and Kathryn being a match literally "made in heaven."

Yes, I know. It's bizarre humor. But it worked for us. It gave us comfort to imagine our two little babies growing up and falling in love…in heaven. When you hurt like this, you take every little bit of comfort you can find.

Although I am healing, I continue to have challenges. Grief strikes in strange moments. I struggle to raise a surviving twin with the constant reminder of what we have lost, intermingled with the guilt of not feeling grateful enough for the fact that I have a healthy surviving baby. I often feel guilty for feeling happy and that I like that life is almost normal again. Often I do not even realize what is weighing heavily on me until it is my turn to speak at my support group, and the words and emotions come flowing out.

I could not do this alone.

You *should* not do this alone.

It took me eight months to finally reach out to a support group. Part of that is because the first three months after Kathryn passed were spent in the Neonatal Intensive Care Unit (NICU) with Charis, hoping and praying that she would survive and thrive. Once she finally came home, she had many special needs and appointments that occupied my time and thoughts.

But once all of that started to calm down, the grief began to emerge.

In late September 2012, I began to search for sponsored activities for Pregnancy and Infant Loss Remembrance Day, on October 15th. In that search, I came across the website for Naomi's Circle, a loss support group created by other mothers who wanted more than just a hospital-sponsored grief support group, but a place where mothers with other children or who hoped to have other children could come and support each other.

In October I attended my first meeting. And as I told my story, I sobbed. Until that moment, I did not realize how much grief and pain I had compartmentalized in order to function and take care of my surviving twin and my other two small children. Once those floodgates opened, they were difficult to stop. This group of women, who fully understood and shared my grief, wrapped their arms around me and showed me they understood.

They really *listened.*

An invisible thread bonds mothers who have lost children. The hugs are knowing, the words are more genuine, and the understanding breaks the isolation. Sometimes it is easier to be comforted by strangers than it is by the people who know us. For me, this is one of those situations. I found more comfort talking with other mothers who have experienced this grief than I ever could with even some of my best friends.

No matter when you lost your baby, you have suffered a trauma, and it will impact you. Maybe not immediately, but at some point you will need to come to terms with the loss. If your community does not have a support group, Facebook has hundreds of groups to support grieving mothers. There are nationwide support organizations for grieving families. Or start your own group in your own.

You have all of us. We are here for you. If you need us, reach out to us. You are not alone.

From my heart to yours,
Alexa

"There is no hurry in grief; be a compassionate, tender friend to yourself. In your grief, do not be hurried...by yourself or anybody else."
—xo, Suzanne

"Over and over I hear, 'There is no right or wrong way to grieve.' Is that really true? What if someone is abusing alcohol or drugs, or not communicating with their partner at all, or thinking of hurting their self or others, or lying in bed for months and months? Are there maybe healthy and unhealthy ways to grieve, with LOTS of room in the healthy range but some clear ideas for unhealthy?"

—Sherokee Ilse

Survival Tip #2: Grieve according to your own needs and your own process.

I Can't Tell You How to Grieve

By Amy Hillis

Sometimes, our life becomes something greater than we ever expected.

Sometimes, that greatness is only achieved through the deepest heartbreak.

My grief is not your grief. I can't presume to know the heartache that you feel. I do know that to experience this pain once in a lifetime is devastating. To experience it more than once? That's just cruel and beyond comprehension. I have experienced this debilitating heartache twice. Once for my son Nathaniel, who passed away in 2001. He was a mere five days old. Then again in 2011 for my son David. He spent five long months in the hospital and lost his fight at eight months old. My grief for Nathaniel was and is still very much a part of me. Fast-forward ten years, add the birth of four more boys, that five-month hospital stay, and the strain of it all on my marriage, and my grief just became exponentially more paralyzing.

This is my story of a life made greater through heartbreak.

Nathaniel was born with citrullinemia, a rare urea-cycle disorder (UCD). Citrullinemia is a genetic disorder, with both parents contributing a damaged gene. Nathaniel's liver was lacking an essential enzyme needed to break down protein. Normally, once protein is broken down, the waste is removed harmlessly through the urine. In the case of a person with a UCD, ammonia is produced instead. This buildup of ammonia in one's system causes brain damage and can be fatal. Nathaniel went into a coma somewhere between day two and day three of life. The buildup of ammonia ultimately caused his death.

I was thirty years old and had no reason to believe I would have a child affected by a genetic disorder, let alone have a child die. I had two older children from my first marriage, and my husband had a daughter from his. The perfect blended family: his, mine, and ours. Except ours was now resting eternally in the baby garden of the local cemetery. As irrational as it sounds, I felt like a failure. I felt solely responsible for his death. I felt lost.

I didn't know how to grieve. I had lost my grandmother when I was twenty, but other than that I had been sheltered from this particular heartache. I didn't know anyone that had lost a child. I didn't belong to a church. The hospital didn't offer any resources on grief. I had a computer and I spent time on the Internet, mostly to read news reports and win auctions on eBay. It never occurred to me to reach out in my grief to others online. Social media as we know it today was nonexistent. I kept my feelings and my grief hidden, particularly from those closest to me. I was stoic in my emotions. I didn't search out support groups. I didn't read books on grief. And I didn't think the heartache was ever going to ease up.

The timing of Nathaniel's death was unique; less than two weeks later, the 9/11 attacks on the World Trade Center happened. Suddenly the whole world was grieving right alongside me.

I spent weeks lying on my couch, glued to my television. I wept, and I raged, and I mourned. And slowly, ever so slowly, I started to live again. I had quit my job prior to Nathaniel being born because I had wanted the opportunity to enjoy his baby years. Instead of nighttime feedings and diaper changes, I spent months watching news reports of the worst terrorist attack on US soil. I learned to grieve vicariously through the stories of those lost in the attack. I learned that if I didn't figure out how to make peace with my heartache, I wouldn't be able to function for my children that still needed their mother.

There is no getting around the fact that grief is messy and unpredictable and makes even the simplest tasks difficult. Laundry, dishes, cooking, spending time with my older children—those are the activities that filled my days. It was a difficult transition from working full time and going to school. I was in the first semester of my master's degree program when I found out I was pregnant with Nathaniel. I had planned on returning once he was born. I was the queen of juggling my time, and suddenly it felt like a life in slow motion. I'm sure to the outside world, it looked like I spent my time doing absolutely nothing, but after losing Nathaniel, it became very clear to me that what others thought was irrelevant.

I needed that time to learn how to live and enjoy life again.

Almost eighteen months to the day after Nathaniel was born, we welcomed our second son into the world. He was healthy, prenatal testing confirmed that, but it didn't stop the worry and anxiety that swirled around my head from the moment he was born. Each one of his milestones was peppered with what-ifs and what-might-have-beens. I had never heard the term "rainbow baby," a term that is used so prevalently these days to describe those babes that are born after loss. The celebration of my rainbow baby was, at times, clouded by the heartache I felt for Nathaniel.

Grief takes up residence in your life. It can lie dormant for long periods of time, and then suddenly it flares up, and you're consumed once again. Events that should be nothing but sunlight and love can trigger episodes of grief and heartache. Yes, I felt happiness and joy, but I let the heartache run alongside each and every joyous occasion. I didn't know any other way. It wasn't until my son David was hospitalized that I was able to turn to the Internet and social media to help me channel my grief.

By the time David was born in May of 2010, I had three young boys at home. I had remained a stay-at-home mom. Through prenatal testing, we knew that two of the boys were going to be affected, like Nathaniel, with citrullinemia. I had met with the surgeons while I was pregnant and learned that the boys would require a liver transplant to "cure" the citrullinemia. So by the time David was born, also with citrullinemia, I had already gone through two liver transplants and numerous hospital stays with the two youngest boys.

David received his liver transplant in August 2010; he was three months old. The liver transplant went well, but he caught a virus post-op and became very ill. I spent five months sitting by his bedside. During that time I was encouraged to write, so I started a blog. Transplanted Thoughts went live on October 22, 2010, roughly a month after David had his transplant. I didn't know how cathartic writing and sharing my story through social media was going to be.

I was naïve during David's hospitalization. After so many hospital stays with my other two sons, I felt confident in the doctor's abilities to pull David through this illness. It wasn't until one of the residents sat me down and had "the talk" with me that I realized I was going to lose another son. Not right away, no. He was still holding his own when she came to talk to me. It was the slap in the face I needed to try and prepare myself with the inevitable. I focused on my writing and the relationships I was forging online.

When I started writing my blog, one of the first things I did was write about Nathaniel. Nine years had passed, and it was the first time I had talked about Nathaniel, albeit virtually. My grief, my guilt, my anger, and my fear had been pushed down deep so I could function in my everyday life. Writing about Nathaniel brought all that raw emotion back to the surface. I poured everything I had into writing, writing updates about David. Writing about what the boys were doing back home. Writing about memories long past. I threw myself into chronicling the events surrounding David's life, and in doing so I created a safe place to share my grief.

David passed away on January 24, 2011 (almost three months after that resident had that talk with me); it was unexpected and traumatic. I had spent five months living in that hospital room, and suddenly I was being evicted without my son. I was crushed. In the wake of his death, I relied on my blog and the steadfast group of people who read it. The support I received through sharing David's life was beyond measure. I was fortunate in those beginning months to have the love and support of people I had never personally met.

The thing that I struggled with the most after David's passing was making the transition from four children to three. I left home one sunny August day with two elementary school kids, a toddler, and a babe, only to return home on a cold winter's day with two elementary school kids and a preschooler. As I mourned the loss of my babe, I was also mourning the growing up of my toddler. I missed being needed. That I-can't-do-anything-for-myself type of need that only a baby or a toddler can provide, 24/7. One of the surgeons had called me a "perpetual caregiver," and he was right; having very young children makes it so. Having very young children with special needs makes it doubly so.

Writing helped fill some of the void, and slowly life took on a new rhythm. A few months after

David's death, one of my online friends asked about organizing a blood drive in his honor. As difficult as it was so soon after his passing, I organized a blood drive for my community and have every April since. It was the beginning of a life made greater through this unbearable heartache.

Life certainly hasn't returned to the way it was before, and for that I am glad. My marriage had suffered—and was suffering—all along. We finally got to that point of knowing it was time to move on. I stopped writing. As cathartic as it was in the months following David's death, it began to feel awkward and forced, so I took a break. I focused on the three young men in my life. I went back to work as an in-home caregiver to a ninety-year-old woman. That's a far cry from the computer programmer and art major I used to be, but it blends much better with the perpetual caregiver inside me. I started going to church; I made new friends. I started living my life on my terms—terms that included raising organ donor awareness and spending as much idle time with my boys as possible.

The heartache? It will always be there. It's a part of me, like my right arm. I am a grieving mother. In two days or forty years, the ache will remain. It's how we tend to that ache that makes the difference between life and a life made greater.

I think the best advice that I can give to you is to find people. Find people, either virtually or in reality, who are willing to listen. It's hard, so very hard, to hit that "publish" button when writing a blog or to call on a friend and say, "Hey, can you spare a few minutes to talk?" Pouring our soul out to another is intrinsically difficult in the best of times, but during our darkest hours, sometimes it's the only way to see daylight again. Maybe your friends and family are struggling as well. Call your pastor, find a support group, or, better yet, create a support group. Find people. And no matter where you are in your journey with grief, the most important thing to remember is to follow your heart. My grief is not your grief; do what feels right to you.

Much Love,
Amy

"Grief isn't linear. It looks different for each person. There is no timeline. There is no right or wrong way to do this. What works for someone else may not help you. Find what does help and cling to it."

—xo, Kelly

The Process of My Grief

By Regina Petsch

I have begun writing this particular snapshot into the most painful part of my life half a hundred times since I was first invited to share a part of my son's story, and I have stopped at the doorway 49 times, with varied reasons as to why it was not a good time to write this. Today I will push past the threshold, and I will willingly walk through the door — the door that I know leads to a place of great pain and sadness. I will walk through it now in the hope of somehow bringing comfort to others. I willingly walk through it now, because I know on the other side of this room of anguish and soul-crushing despair, there is hope.

This is a snapshot into my experience. I am no writer. I am no professional book contributor. I'm not even sure I am a good blogger, but I am a mother who has been there. I am a mother who honestly was not certain she would survive the experience of losing her son. I am a mother who certainly never believed there would be life after his death, much less hope or happiness.

This would be and should be my son's seventh end of summer; at the beginning of fall, he should be starting first grade, riding the big yellow bus with his big brother. I can see in my mind's eye how he would look. I can imagine how his voice would sound. How his laughter would echo across our backyard.

But none of that has ever happened. We have celebrated six would-be/should-be birthdays, complete with candles, cake, and balloons, but we are celebrating with a tiny urn. One that contains the ashes of a tiny boy and the remnants of his mother's broken dreams — and a piece of her very soul.

I had been previously married and had two daughters relatively easily. In my second marriage I was officially diagnosed with "secondary infertility". We tried for a very long time to have children. We suffered years of disappointment and two first-trimester miscarriages. We tried everything known to us to conceive and carry a baby, and when all else failed and seven years had passed, we tried IVF. Low and behold, it worked, and we had our first son. When he was almost two, we tried again, and after a grueling and difficult time, we found success a second time.

My pregnancy with William was difficult, but I can honestly say it was the happiest time in my life. I could not see how life could get any better. Nothing in the world could have prepared me for that horrific day in May when all hope of him surviving disappeared. It was with the anger and hate of a thousand burning suns that I delivered my second son into the world, but once he was here — tiny, perfect in every way and alive — the anger disappeared (though it would return later). In that hospital room, holding my second miracle son, there was only love.

Despite great odds and extreme prematurity, William lived. For exactly one hour and forty-seven minutes, he lived. He was pronounced dead in the arms of his father. Later after everyone had gone home, I was alone in the hospital room with my tiny boy. I tried desperately to memorize every single one of his tiny features. I took hundreds of pictures~ pictures meant to last a lifetime. Pictures that now reside in a tiny box and are forever burned into my memory. When there was no other choice, I let the kind nurse wash and dress his tiny body, take his measurements and footprints, and take him away to the morgue. To this day, I still wish I would have held him just a little bit longer. But in my heart, I know it could never have been long enough.

The first few days after his death, I remember feeling mostly just numb. It was as if the true horror and pain would be too much to bear, and in self-defense, my body was just numb. I found myself giving comfort to others. There were streams of people with sad faces, crying, not knowing what to say to me. Hundreds of platitudes meant to bring comfort. Numbness I was grateful for.

Walking the long walk down the aisle of our church on the day of his funeral, the numbness disappeared. I remember standing at the end of the aisle screaming: "I cannot do this. You cannot make me do this." God, I felt as if my heart was actually splitting in two. I felt as if the pain would surely kill me. And in truth, I felt like I wanted to die. If my son could not live, then I did not want to either. Thankfully that feeling eventually passed, though I can't say exactly when it did.

The first few weeks after his death were, by far, the very hardest of my life. I was lost. My heart and soul were shattered. I was blessed to have living children, but when people said that I should not grieve because at "least you have living children," the rage truly set in.

My husband's grandfather, who I loved more than if he were my own grandfather, had lost three of his four children. They had all lived to be adults, but all died tragically young. I could not even begin to imagine someone standing next to the coffin of his second daughter, who was but twenty-four when a ruptured brain aneurysm took her life, and trying to comfort him by saying, "Well, don't be sad — you have three other kids." *Why, then, would people say such a thing to a mother who lost a baby?*

I learned the hard way that people often say things meant to bring comfort, but in reality, the words are like a hot knife into an already shattered heart.

It was in some suspended state between rage and despair that I lived those first few weeks and months. I wanted to know why. Why is my baby dead? Why is the child I wanted and prayed for dead while so many unwanted babies are alive and being mistreated? Why did God allow me to get pregnant if I was only going to lose the baby? Why was this happening to me? What had I done to deserve this? How am I supposed to survive this? Oddly enough finding out years later *why* I went into pre-term labor did very little to ease my pain.

I yelled; I swore; I cried. I railed at God, I screamed at the universe, I crawled into a deep dark pit of despair, and, for a while, I lost complete hope that I would ever be happy again.

The God's honest truth of the matter is that I could not climb out of that deep, dark pit alone. I was nowhere near strong enough to climb out. In fact, I was weaker and more vulnerable than I can ever remember being—and that pissed me off, too. I felt that surely no one else had ever felt this level of soul-crushing grief and survived.

Though I auto-piloted my way through the first weeks and months, when the curtain lifted and I was there standing seemingly naked and alone in my pit, the sadness nearly overwhelmed me.

And then I remembered. I remembered that my very own sister-in-law had lost her baby just two weeks before her due date. I remembered the words she said to me afterward. Suddenly I was absolutely desperate to talk to women who had survived. Some innate survival skill kicked in—I do not know how or why—but I knew I needed to seek out other women who had been here in this black hole pit of absolute despair—and survived to tell the tale. I was lucky to have a local group that met monthly. I attended my first "Empty Arms" meeting, and, for the very first time in months, I allowed myself the tiniest sliver of hope that I would, in fact, survive this nightmare.

I also sought out professional help. I knew that feeling like I wanted to die was not a good thing. I knew that in truth I had lots to live for, not the least of which was my near two-year-old son who needed his mommy. But I was at an all-time low, and I could not get out. I went to "talk therapy," and for the first time in my life I started on an antidepressant medication.

I was so angry that I *had* to take a maternity leave when I had no baby to care for. I mean, what in the ever-loving hell did they expect me to do for six weeks?

And then, the fateful day, my first day back at work. Just so happened that I returned to work on the very same day as a coworker who had also been on maternity leave—only her son was alive, and mine was dead. And just when I thought the anger and pure rage had peaked, it went a little higher and multiplied by a thousand.

How could it be that the world just carried on? My personal world had shattered; I was thrown into chaos and despair. Never, *ever* would it be the same again. How could the rest of the world go on, seemingly unaffected?

Ever so gradually, the fog began to lift in the pit; I did not notice it at first. In a giant leap of Faith we tried IVF again~ after a devastating failed cycle~ we found success. The pregnancy was horrific from the start~ my most difficult ever. Hard to explain feeling both great joy and paralyzing grief simultaneously. Again my water broke early: 20weeks and 3days. They offered to "terminate" my pregnancy. I replied with more strength than I knew I had with: OH HELL NO. Losing William gave me the strength to fight for his baby sister. I simply could not fathom having another funeral and another tiny urn filled with the ashes of another dearly loved and wanted child. William's baby sister, Faith, was born at 24weeks

3days~ and is now a healthy, happy and whole 5 year old.

Here's the double-edged sword of a grieving mother's heart. Months later when I smiled a genuine smile and laughed a genuine laugh (as opposed to the forced smiles and fake, uncomfortable laughter I'd been displaying for months), it felt wrong. It felt really, really, *really* wrong. Guilt such as I have never known seized me. Instantly I felt like I was somehow betraying my son. How dare I be happy even for a moment, when he is dead? And so goes the dance of despair. One step forward. Four steps back. It is a club no mother would willingly join. It is a process, not an event. It was as if I had to relearn how to live.

I know I will never, ever be the woman and mother I was before William died. Somehow I'd like to think that he has helped me become a better version of myself. But the road to get here was fraught with trauma, guilt, heartache, despair, and, at times, pure anguish.

Last year, a full five-and-a-half years after his birth, brief life, and untimely death, I began writing his story. I felt I needed to get his story out of my head. I felt driven to reach out to others who had also lost children.

So here I sit. To paraphrase, it is said that writing is easy; one need only sit at your keyboard and bleed. Seven years later, I can neither write nor read William's story without bleeding from the heart. I still cry. Every. Single. Time.

If I could speak to myself in the early days of his loss, I'm uncertain what I would say. Thousands of words were said to me, and very few brought comfort.

In speaking to you now, I can only tell you what I have learned from the death of my son:

- Mommies and daddies often grieve very differently.

- Your grief will be unique to YOU. There is no "right" way~ we each must find our own path back to hope.

- What worked for me may very well be useless for others.

- In the pit of despair, when all hope seemed lost, I was comforted to be in the company of people who had survived losing a child.

- Sometimes it is best to just be with someone when they are grieving. Words are not always necessary.

- Sometimes people's words unintentionally hurt when they were meant to comfort.

- Sometimes medical help is needed to get through the worst of the grief. It does not mean that I am weak; it means I am strong enough to know when I cannot do it alone.

- As painful as his loss was, I am eternally grateful that I was chosen to be his mother, even though that gratitude took *years* to feel.

- I can survive things that I thought would surely kill me.

- There will always be a William-shaped hole in my mommy heart, imprinted on my soul.

- Grieving the loss of my child is a lifelong process, not an event.

• I am right where I am supposed to be in this process of grief.

But today I have hope. Today I know that he lived and died for a higher purpose, though the fullness of that has yet to be revealed. Today I can *choose* to seek happiness and hope in my daily life. I can't promise you that this will ever be *easy~* but I can promise that it *will not* always be *this* hard.

With profound empathy, love and light,
Regina

"It's okay to ask for help. It's okay to say, 'I need to talk about this,' or 'I can't talk about this right now.' It's okay to be a little selfish and do whatever you need to in order to make it through the day."

—AnnMarie G

Grief is like a War

By Wendy R. Smith

On Wednesday, April 21, 2010, the world as we knew it fell completely apart. We discovered one of our babies, at 23 weeks' gestation, was dead. We were pregnant with twins; they were suffering from a cruel disease called Twin to Twin Transfusion Syndrome (TTTS). Just three weeks prior, we'd traveled to USC to undergo laser surgery to save their lives. On April 1st, there were two heartbeats!

During a routine checkup ultrasound twenty days later, we learned of Baby A's demise. Our doctor could not find both heartbeats. What ensued included an awful and awkward discussion, several hours and days of shock, crying, numbness, and many horrific memories I've struggled to forget. Life, since that day, has never been the same. The worst part was having to tell people Alex was gone.

Every April 21st is known as Alex's "angelversary" to our family. We try not to think of it as the day one of our babies died, but the day one of our babies became an angel! We honor and memorialize our sweet boy and linger on the precious memories we have. On that very day, we captured beautiful pictures of Alex and Zach in utero, more memories which are always, although bittersweet, nonetheless cherished. We also had two lovely sketches made of the twins together, both Angel Alexander and Survivor Zachary, based on what Alex would have looked like, since they are identical. Both A and Z have big blue eyes, soft blond hair, and incredibly handsome smiles. I always find comfort when I imagine them together. We try to savor their "twin-ness." Zachary knows he's a twin, and this is a fact we are all proud of. His older brother also knows we have a guardian angel. And this always makes my heart smile (even though I still get choked up at times).

Many who've shared similar grief journeys say that when their baby died, they felt a part of themselves die. There is no better way to describe the shock and anguish of such loss. That moment forever changes who we are. No matter what you do or what you say, no amount of pleading with God, no magic pill, no nothing, will ever bring your baby back. So, we begin to establish a whole new reality from that day forward.

We continued carrying the pregnancy for five more lifesaving weeks, until May 28th, when the pain of preterm labor struck. I was bleeding heavily, and Zachary was already making his way for the exit! Both boys were delivered by an emergent C-section. Zachary came at 11:06 a.m., and then Alexander quietly arrived at 11:07. Zachary Alexander, the greatest miracle I've ever known, was wheeled right off to the NICU in his special high-tech crib with his entourage of neonatal specialists. He weighed only 1 pound 11 ounces, and there are no words to describe what a marvel he is — he really is a superhero! And at the same time, I'm overwhelmed with the show of love my oldest son has for his little brother.

I'm contributing to this important body of stories because I want to share how this experience has transformed us. Above all, I've come to the realization that we're not alone in this grief journey. To anyone and everyone who experiences such loss, you must know you are not alone! We, every one of us who has gone through this, are part of this crazy club which some call "baby-loss moms." It used to suck being part of this club; in fact, people thought you were bat$h*t crazy. That's no longer the case. Today, I'm a very proud member! And so are many of my friends! I once had a dad at daycare look at me like I had three boobs when I told him my baby has an angel twin. It just feels so foreign to people who are not part of our special club.

I've learned to adapt. I began to navigate through the pain associated with this loss. There is so much involved in the aftermath and all that's happened in the wake of his death. There were so many emotions, and so many hurdles, but the bottom line is this: it can be overcome. The best thing that worked for me was to talk (or to write) about my experience. The more you talk, the more it begins to make sense. I tell the story like a war story because that, to me, is exactly what it is. I went on to publish the story of our twins, including a summary of how we, as a family, survived the experience. And I must say that there has been no substitute for the therapeutic effect telling our story has had on my heart.

Most importantly, I was able to connect with other families who experienced similar battles. In fact, I connected with a very special someone who went on to found the TTTS Support Team. We send care packages to families all over the world affected by TTTS. My friend and I have our TTTS stories in common, one survivor and one angel, but we have so much more in common, too. I'm not kidding when I say she's the sister I never had. And I'm quite sure she will say the same of me.

I honestly trust that God is in control, and He knows what He's doing. This doesn't mean it's always easy, though. But things really are starting to come full circle. My husband and I are now able to laugh about things that used to make us cry. And we are getting closer as a result of things that we used to let pull us apart.

The grief I've experienced has evolved as the last three years have gone by. For the first year, especially while I was still pregnant with the twins, and while visiting our survivor in the NICU, I was just numb! That's the only way to explain how I felt. And I know now that's how grief works. In order to protect myself and so I could still function, I just walked around like a zombie with no feelings. Sometimes I got sick to my stomach, usually when I saw identical twins or heard either a happy baby story or a horrific story of loss. My body still tried to function, but my heart just didn't know how to at that point.

Then around the first anniversary of the loss (also known as his "angelversary"), I started trying to make sense of Alex's death, and I began frantically trying to do something special to memorialize him. A few things worked to help me, other than writing, including realizing that grief is like a living thing and can't be ignored or denied. I had to acknowledge the loss. Choosing to stand up and speak out loud about my experience has helped even more than writing about it. It has helped give me closure, instead of just pretending none of this ever happened. Certainly there was therapy and pharmaceutical intervention involved as well.

After lots of legwork to find a local bereavement support group meeting, I participated in my first "Walk to Remember Our Babies" event in October 2011. I connected with other families who stood up in a circle, held hands, and told the stories of their babies. I have since gone on to become more involved in our local bereavement support group, and I help organize this walk each October. When we get together and talk about our angels, I feel like I'm comfortable, accepted, and much more than that old, crazy Prozac momma.

Each mother has a different story. There's one thing we all have in common, though; *we all know the ache of loss.* We all left the hospital with empty arms. Some of us have death certificates for our babies. Some of us have their ashes. Some of us visit them at their grave. Some of us believe they are angels and that we'll be reunited again someday. Some of us just know they're gone. It's as if their absence is a living being, always there, especially on milestones and/or holidays. Some of us count these babies when asked, "How many kids do you have?" Some of us do not, because it's just too painful and confusing.

When Zachary was born, I fell in love with this sweet baby-blue stuffed lamb from the hospital gift shop, and it says a prayer. He was perched near

Zachary's bedside the whole time he was in the hospital. In fact, the nighttime NICU nurses took a photo of Zach with this lambkin, and it blows me away how teeny he was! He still loves his lambkin to this day. God forbid something should happen to that smelly little creature (it's almost like he's a "stand-in" for Alex).

Just last Sunday, I decided to move him up to Alex's corner in Zach's room. We've got this corner shelf for them in Zachary's room. Alex's ashes are in a little wooden cube urn we picked out for him. It says "Baby Alexander—Our little Angel, May 28, 2010," and it really looks like a baby block with a ducky on one side, ABC blocks on another, and a teddy bear on the other side. As much as I hate the fact that we have the cremated remains of our baby on a shelf, I'm starting to come to peace with it all. This corner houses all the little items in tribute to our twins. Each of these little trinkets means so much to me. Each is a memento which helps soften the regret and angst held over the loss of Alexander's life.

My biggest regret is that I didn't spend time holding him after he was born. I wish I would have taken a time-out and held him and kissed him and experienced him. I told myself I wanted to remember him the way he was while he was alive. But then I missed that opportunity to really say good-bye. That, I regret. I believe, like I said before, that he's still with us, in spirit form, but it still aches. It will never feel right.

The whole thing was just so horrendous, from the trauma of a preterm birth to being at the NICU, and having to call the funeral home to make arrangements for Alex. And I feel the need to vomit when I see a picture of the doctor who confirmed Alex's death. Sometimes I feel like it's all made me jaded; I had transformed into someone creepy who nobody wanted to be around. Fortunately, I know that to be different now, but it still hurts. It still pains me each time I drive by that funeral home. And when I really think about it, it hurts. It hurts to know we'll never get to see our twins grow up together. Sometimes it hurts so badly, it feels like it's too much, but then I get my head screwed on straight again, and I realize it does get better. Time has helped heal. And I hope the same is true for you!

I have ten important beliefs I'd like to share with you. I hope these beliefs help you as much as they've helped me:

I believe you are **never** alone.

I believe the power is within us to make each day as beautiful or as crappy as we choose. Life is filled with ups and downs, but it's important to recognize the power of positive internal dialogue.

I believe we'll be reunited with our babies someday! No doubt about it.

I believe it's important not to take a moment of this life for granted.

I believe it helps to count your blessings.

I believe someday you'll realize you're stronger than you ever thought you were.

I believe in laughing as hard as you can, whenever you can. My sick sense of humor has saved me countless times, literally. And it feels so good to laugh through tears.

I believe sometimes there's nothing better to do than have a good cry. Sometimes you just have to.

Perhaps one thing might be better: take a nap.

I believe in angels. And when in doubt, see #1.

And one more thing: please keep in mind that grief is a journey, and certain days will hit you harder than others. Once in a while, I just have a day, out of the clear blue sky, where I want to cry. Or I just feel bitchy. Lately, I've had a few of those days in a row, and with all of life's stresses thrown at me, I feel unfocused, but I do know it will get better. It is only temporary. I may feel anxious and mad and/or sad, but it will subside. I know this to be true.

Finally, the ability of a true, understanding, and genuine friend who listens can make all the difference! Please know this: even if you feel you don't have a friend in the world, or not a soul who understands your pain, you're wrong! Sometimes I tell myself this to get myself out of my personal pity party, but usually I say it because it just makes my heart feel at peace. We'll always miss our babies, no matter what, but I got to the point where my sorrow and depression over losing Alex was taking away from the present joy with my other amazing boys (not to mention my amazing husband). Sending lots of love, support, and encouragement, from my heart to yours. And warm hugs from my arms to yours...

Shared with love,
Wen

"Everything you're feeling is normal.
You're not going crazy. You will never go
back to your old normal, but you will find
a new one that you are comfortable with.
You will survive. You're not alone."

—Kristi Bothur

Survival Tip #3: Don't expect a timeline, and don't let others put a timeline on your grieving process.

Tiny Angel

By Starr Bryson

Fifteen years ago, I experienced what no parent should ever have to. I lost my son. This is not how life is supposed to be; no parent should ever have to bury their own child. It is not the natural order of life, and it is not what any of us ever expect to have to survive.

He was just three months old, and it was far too soon. I wasn't done loving him. We had so many memories yet to make. I never saw him walk or heard him talk.

When a child dies, it is more than just the life that dies. It is a future that dies. All the hopes and dreams of a life unlived — these die, too.

I fell in love with him when he was still inside my womb. I read Dr. Seuss aloud to my blossoming stomach and I sang to him, and when he was still safely living inside of my protective body, I told him what a wonderful life he was going to have.

When he was born, he was absolutely perfect. He was beautiful. I held him, I breastfed him, and I changed his diapers. I loved him, cuddled him, and kissed him. I sang to him, and I read to him. I was twenty years old, and I had no idea what I was doing. But this tiny human, he was all mine; he was everything that is right in the world. He was the best part of me.

I had not celebrated Christmas for seven years prior to 1998, due to a very tragic event in my childhood that made Christmas painful, nearly unbearable. I simply ignored it as if it was any other month, any other day.

Until I had Tiny Angel. I knew he was too young to know the difference and would never remember his first Christmas. But it was important to me to start with his first Christmas. To begin my healing with this new life, to love and learn how to celebrate Christmas again. Because when he was older, I wanted Christmas to be beautiful and magical for him.

For the first time in seven years, I put up a Christmas tree. Everything was blue. For Tiny Angel. I spent entirely too much money on gifts that would never matter to an infant, and I wrapped them and put them under our tree.

I scheduled an appointment to have his photos taken with Santa. I even bought him a new outfit for the occasion.

And on the day of this appointment, when I woke up from our nap, he didn't. I tried to resuscitate him. I called 911 and told them my son wasn't breathing. I kept trying CPR, but I knew. I knew in that deepest part of my heart, where all of our darkest fears lie, it was too late. So I held him close to me and rocked him while I sobbed.

The paramedics had to throw themselves against the door to get into my apartment because I would not get up from the floor. I would not relinquish my hold on my baby. They had to pry him from my fingertips. I ran after them to the ambulance, swinging my fists and screaming. They were not taking my baby from me! I would fight them all. I punched an officer in the face before I was restrained and subdued with tranquilizers.

A very nice cop sat on the ground next to me where I lay in the driveway, now subdued but oh so heartbroken. It wasn't true; it couldn't be true. I lay there on the hard ground and wished for the earth to open up and swallow me. This police officer sat with me until my husband was able to get home.

The rest of the night is a blur. A horrible, mind-numbing, heart-shattering blur. I cried so hard, I cried so much, and I kept saying, "I want him back — please give him back." I sobbed into the late hours of the night and even after the sun rose over the horizon, bringing with it a new day I didn't want to live for.

Thankfully my mother and in-laws were able to fly to North Carolina during this time and stay with us. Because I was a mess and couldn't even take care of myself, the parentals took over and planned the funeral, met with the funeral director, and took care of all of those details for us. I picked out the outfit I wanted him buried in and placed it with his favorite binky and blankie for my father-in-law to take to the funeral home.

I wanted nothing to do with any of it.

I will never forget the evening my mother-in-law found all of the bottles in the fridge of pre-pumped breast milk. She just stood there, with the fridge door hanging open, and stared at them while she cried. She then systematically took them one by one to the sink and dumped their contents, and she cried the entire time. The memory of her standing over the sink, crying for my son, is forever burned in my mind.

His funeral was five days after his passing because there was an investigation. The coroner that signed his death certificate "did not believe in SIDS" and therefore ruled his death as accidental asphyxiation.

On a cold and rainy day, heavy with black clouds underneath a gray sky, we gathered to say good-bye to my Tiny Angel. On Christmas Eve, when other families gathered around a tree with their loved ones, we gathered around a hole in the ground. I sat on an unforgiving, cold metal chair and stared at the oh-so-tiny coffin. A blue box with my son inside.

I cried through the entire service with gut-wrenching sobs; I don't remember a thing that was said. I was that lady, that cliché from the movies, and I tried to throw myself into the hole on top of that little blue box.

When we got home, I was so infuriated, so angry at the world, so angry for what I had lost, I picked that Christmas tree up and threw it through the living room window. In a manic state, I ripped the wrapping off of every single present, tore them apart, and tossed it all out the window. I wanted to throw myself out that window, right through the jagged pieces of glass.

Because no matter how hard I cried, no matter how much I cried, I could not cry out the broken pieces of my heart, and it hurt. It hurt so damn much. I swore off a God I don't even believe in; I swore off Christmas. I wanted to die. The pain was just too big, too much.

It has been fifteen long years since what I loved so much was lost to me. There is not a single day that I don't think about Tiny Angel. I wonder about who he would be, what he would look like. Would he like to read and write, like me and his little brother? Would he talk a lot and make beautiful art like his baby brother? Would he play soccer? Would he be taller than me? There are many what-ifs and could-have-beens, and I'll just never know.

I long to hold him just one more time. I yearn to put my arms around my little baby boy who left this world far too early. Just once more, to have him against me, to smell his baby smell and rock him to sleep while I sing to him. I would give anything.

Every single day I think about him, miss him, and love him.

Grieving is a long and winding road, one I wish I didn't have to travel. There is still a piece of my heart that is broken over my baby boy, a piece that will never heal. I will never be done grieving for that beautiful baby boy.

Hugs,
Starr B.

Chapter 2: Raising Other Children While or After Dealing with Loss

Whether or not to tell your other children if you have experienced a loss or if a sibling is dying can be a very difficult decision. The contributors to this book have a varied outlook on this topic, mostly due to the ages of our other children at the time of the loss, or the point at which the loss occurred. We hope this chapter provides help if you are struggling on what and how to tell the other children.

Secondly, if you are a parent with a terminally ill child, trying to find the way to explain to them that he or she is dying can be extraordinarily difficult. We have some information on this topic as well, but sadly, as Sheila Q pointed out, there are few good resources on this topic.

I had two other children when I was pregnant with my twins. My son was four, and our other daughter was almost two. On one of our many trips home from visiting our maternal-fetal manager and having our weekly ultrasound, usually with an increasingly worse outlook for the fate of our babies, my husband and I discussed how much worse this would be on us emotionally if this experience had occurred during our first pregnancy. At the time, we had no idea how terrible the pain would actually be of losing one or both of our twins, but we felt certain that the fact that we had two other children at home would at least soften the crushing blow of our loss.

I do not know how I would have survived the first few weeks after we lost Kathryn without my other children. My sweet Ella literally saved me from falling into a deep depression in those first few days and weeks after Kathryn died. At not even two years old, she was so perceptive, loving, and concerned.

I will never forget the day that I opened the small package with Kathryn's effects, sent home from the NICU. I sobbed as I held up the tiny blood pressure cuff my daughter had worn for two days. Ella, who had been playing on the other side of the room, grabbed a napkin and walked over to the couch. She climbed up in my lap, patted dry my tears and said, in her sweet voice, "Oh goodness sake, Mommy."

Those sweet words. A baby, comforting me like an adult. Better than an adult. And I was overwhelmed with relief and love for that tiny little creature.

Even though she could comfort me, she did not really understand why I was sad or what was happening. She knew that I had been in the hospital and had babies in my belly, but that was about all she could possibly comprehend.

Our four-year-old son, on the other hand, knew something was wrong. He clearly understood that I had had two babies in my belly. He knew and understood that the babies were sick enough that his mommy had to live at the hospital for over a month before the babies came. And he knew that he was supposed to have *two* babies coming home.

It was heartbreaking when my husband explained to Braedan that Kathryn was too sick and had gone to heaven; we would only have one baby coming home. Braedan yelled out at my husband and called him a liar.

"You're lying! We're supposed to have two babies!"

He could not understand.

At that point, part of me truly wished that we had told him more about their illness and prepared him better. I wish that he had been able to see Kathryn so that she would be more than just a photograph to him. But not everyone would want to follow that course of action.

Over the last two years, my older children have talked a lot about Kathryn. I find it comforting that they remember her, think about her, and miss her. It is not unusual for one of them to randomly bring her up in conversation, or ask questions about where she is and why. I am glad that we have been so open with them.

We recently had a burial service for Kathryn. My children were very involved, to the extent that they even helped me paint a wooden box for her ashes and some keepsakes. I am so glad that we were able to include them and help them say good-bye in a way that was uplifting and encouraging. The little ones are so intuitive and so full of questions.

Next, Heather shares her story of how they told her two older children, and following this contribution, we share differing perspectives from several other contributors on how and when or if they told their children.

"My grief was like a popcorn machine. I kept a lid on it until I couldn't anymore and it would spill over."

—Rachel R.

Survival Tip #4: You are the only one who can decide how/when/if to tell the other children about your loss, and do not feel pressured to do what someone else did.

As Long As We Remember Her

By Heather O'Brien Webb

The hardest thing I have ever had to do was tell my older daughters that their baby sister had died.

I was 42 weeks and 3 days pregnant when our third daughter, Clara Edith, was born still on July 1, 2012. She had been moving and kicking only a day and a half before, when I went into labor, and we did not foresee the terrible news that we would hear from the admitting staff at the hospital.

"We can't find her heartbeat." Time stood still. We hoped and prayed and begged that they would be wrong. I believed, until the moment I saw her beautiful, still face, that they would be wrong.

But the doctors were not wrong. My husband and I were suddenly faced with a completely different reality from the one we planned; the new reality included two excited girls who had waved good-bye to us as and were now expecting to meet their baby sister. I will never forget their happy faces when they bounded into my hospital room. "Where's the baby, Mom? Can I hold her first?"

I asked them to sit at the foot of my hospital bed, and I told them that something sad had happened. Our baby girl had developed an infection while she was inside of my belly, and she had died. Her heart had stopped beating, and she could not be saved.

Our ten-year-old hugged me and cried into my shoulder. Our stoic nine-year-old rubbed my ankle and stared off into space. She climbed into David's lap, appearing emotionless but allowing herself to be folded into his arms.

We decided not to allow the girls to see Clara. I didn't want them to remember her that way. The photographer was able to take beautiful, tasteful black-and-white photographs of our sweet girl, and our older girls looked at these pictures and commented on how beautiful she was, and how much she looked like them.

The next day, our nine-year-old crawled into my hospital bed and began crying as she put her arms around my neck.

"Remember I said I didn't want a baby sister? Is that why Clara died?"

It was a heartbreaking moment. I held her close and told her that her words could not have changed what happened to our baby, not for good or for bad. She nodded and wiped her tears. We hugged for a long time, the crisis past, but the pain still lingering.

On the night after I was released from the hospital, I was tucking the girls into bed when our oldest asked me about cremation. She had heard us discussing our meeting with the funeral director, and she wanted to know what would happen to her baby sister. She was very upset at the idea that Clara would be "burned." We explained that it would only be her sister's body that would be cremated, and the part of Clara that we love was her soul, her personality, her spirit. We told her that Clara's soul and spirit were with us, inside us. As long as we remember and love her, she will always be with us.

In the wake of that difficult conversation, our daughters suggested we find as many ways as possible to remember our baby, to make sure that other people remember her name and her story. In the year since Clara died, we have worked together as a family to honor her memory.

Just before Clara's first birthday, I asked our friends and family to write or photograph Clara's name in unique ways. Our older girls' were among the most creative and heartfelt. They have helped me cut and sew tiny cloth diapers for the Teeny Tears service organization, which provides tiny flannel diapers to hospitals and bereavement support organizations for families that have suffered the loss of a preemie or micro-preemie. My girls helped choose colors of yarn for blankets for the hospital where Clara was born, and have learned to knit to make blankets of their own.

Our family has performed countless random acts of kindness in Clara's memory; each one helps keep her alive for us and within us. It doesn't remove the pain of losing her, and nothing ever will, but it gives us a purpose and a way to channel our loss into helping and encouraging others who walk beside us on this painful road.

With Hope,
Heather

"Tova, I love the way you explained that 'their hearts and souls were very real' but that their bodies weren't strong. That's a beautiful explanation."

—Sandi H.

Chapter 3: When They Don't Know What to Say...

As a society, we are inept at handling loss, especially pregnancy and infant loss. Mothers are left feeling that their losses do not count or were otherwise insignificant. Many mothers have been severely hurt and even offended by the thoughtless words that come out of people's mouths after a woman has lost her baby or child. And worse, they have been made to feel like their loss (especially early losses) did not matter.

This is not a judgment against anyone. Truthfully, before our loss, I did not comprehend the grief that accompanies even such early losses. I would do things so differently for people that I know had lost a baby...

Finding the "right" words to say to a grieving mother is a topic that I blog about from time to time, because it truly is amazing how many awful things I have heard said to a grieving mother. And I believe it is something that we are just simply uneducated about. Because unless you have been there, it is so hard to understand the emotions. I'll never forget the comment left on my blog when I wrote about this topic. She said, "I would add: 'Do not say, as a friend said to me when my twelve-year-old died, You need to get a puppy'"!" Oh my word!

I believe that a large part of the "Breaking the Silence" campaign—the campaign in the "loss community" to end the "silence" around pregnancy and infant loss—should be focused on educating others on what is appropriate to say and do. But the difficulty lies in the fact that not everyone is comforted by the same things. I thought I had it all figured out when I wrote a post entitled, "How to Help a Friend Survive the First Year After Pregnancy or Infant Loss," and I was even more proud when the online magazine *Still Standing* featured this post. However, I got knocked down a notch or two when I read some of the comments by other grieving mothers who replied that some of my suggestions were the *worst* advice. I had to amend my post with the caveat that these were suggestions that worked for me and those in my circle of grieving mothers that I had spoken with, but you know the mother in question, and not all of these suggestions may be appropriate.

As another example of the difficulty in comforting a grieving parent, when I have been asked by others what is appropriate to say to a grieving mother, I always tell them that you cannot go wrong by saying, "I am sorry." Well, it turns out that is not always true, either. I was scanning through comments on one of my grief support groups the other day and saw this posted:

Two-plus years out and I'm still not comfortable responding to "I'm sorry for your loss." "Thank you" just feels wrong. I kinda want to say, "Yeah. Me too." But that comes across rude and I really don't want to do that—these are well-meaning friends and acquaintances, and they aren't saying stupid things, like "at least you have one," simply that they're sorry.

However, even though some may still be bothered by this, I still stand by my belief that if you cannot think of anything at all to say, "I'm sorry for your loss" is one of the least offensive comments. And moms, if you don't want to say thank you to that, just say "I appreciate that." Because I'm sure, someplace deep down, you do appreciate the fact that people are thinking of you and are sorry for you. It's so hard for people to know what to say and do. But they want to do something. I'd much rather have people telling me that they are sorry than just completely ignoring it, like the loss never happened. Because your loss matters.

There are also those people who "get it" and do their best to help you. Some people, whether they have suffered a similar loss or not, just seem to have a knack for doing and saying the most helpful things. We wanted to make sure those acts of kindness were recognized as well, so those are highlighted at the end of this chapter.

"There are two types of people: those who will know what to say and do, and those who don't. It's not entirely their fault and has little to do with how close you were before. You're an unwilling initiate of a private club, and those who are not members don't understand the rules."

—Jennie Goutet

Survival Tip #5: Be ready for the fact that people want to help, but sometimes say dumb things.

The Things People Say

By Suzanne M. Tucker

When I lost my first baby, I judged myself for the pain my body wanted to take me into. I was scared that if allowed it to, sadness might swallow me whole.

That first miscarriage blindsided me. I was lying on the ultrasound table and turned to look at my doctor's face just in time to see it go flat. I turned back to the screen to search for that little blinking light, but I couldn't find it. My doctor had stopped looking at the screen. He was talking to me.

"One in four pregnancies. Your age..." His words flew over my head as I concentrated my efforts on breathing and holding back the tears (which fell anyway).

I sat there a long time. I didn't want to get off the table. I didn't want to get dressed or walk through the waiting room. I didn't want this to be real.

We had a D & C and named our son Leo. Days turned into weeks, and I continued to hurt. I resented the promise that time would heal all wounds. *Where was my healing, and how long was this going to take?* I wondered. I judged myself for the pain I was suffering. *"One in four pregnancies"? Are you kidding me?! Where are all the other hurting moms? I must not be handling this well.*

I became increasingly embarrassed by how deep my wounds ran. I wanted to be faithful. I wanted to be hopeful. I wanted to embody the sort of grace strong women (or whom I judged to be "strong women") embodied when they faced impossible things, accepting the unacceptable in stride. Instead I hurt. And though it still felt to me like time should be standing still, the sun kept rising and setting. Weeks passed, and I raced to catch up with life. "Soldier on," I told myself, echoing back what I felt the world around me was saying. I hoped busyness held the key to making my pain go away. The pull to stay a body in motion was strong, but it didn't take me long to realize that even perpetual doing wasn't going to make this hurt go away.

Over a month later, a friend called to check on me. She asked me how I was doing, to which I answered with the standard "I'm fine." But my friend heard past this half-truth and gently pressed me further. With compassion in her voice, she told me how very sorry she was for the early end to our pregnancy and loss of our baby. It was more in the things she didn't say than what she did and the way she listened that told me I could let my guard down. I felt safe to share myself and the things that weighed heaviest on my heart. When we got off the phone, my tears fell as fresh and as fast as if I were still there, lying on the ultrasound table. And then, something else happened. Inside myself, I realized a small but very real comfort rising up from within me. I was still hurting, yes, but this experience taught me something. It was in slowing down and moving closer to my loss, not further from it, that I began to heal.

As one miscarriage turned into two, two turned into three, and three turned into four and then five, I discovered that contrary to popular belief, words could be thrown like sticks and stones, and words could hurt, but at the same time I realized that words could help me heal.

In time spent alone, reading, praying, and journaling, and in time spent with others, talking, listening, and sharing, thoughts and words and little moments full of great love wrapped around my hurting heart like a bandage.

"How are you doing?"

"I've been thinking of you."

"We are praying for you."

"I am so sorry. I am so, so sorry."

Others would give that knowing look that required no words at all.

I quickly learned that the experiences that were helping me heal came with words and actions from myself and others that allowed me to have my own experience, whatever that may be. In words like the ones above, I felt compassion. In asking, listening, receiving, and sharing, my heart continued to heal.

I learned to watch for other things as well that did not allow me my experience so that I could do my best to avoid them. After hearing things like, "They are in a better place," and "At least you have other children," responses to someone learning about my losses, my body would immediately react with some sort of tightness or discomfort, and I would get still and quiet. I'd feel my experiences, and indeed my very self, being dismissed, and though likely meant to bring me comfort, what I heard in these words instead was, "Plenty of other people have known losses far greater than your own. Isn't it time for you be done grieving?"

In the midst of comments like, "It wasn't meant to be," "They are in a better place," and "God doesn't make mistakes," I struggled. These sentiments left me feeling not loved or supported, but judged. They said to me: "Where's your faith? Things could be worse. Count yourself lucky. Why aren't you past this? Why aren't you feeling grateful instead?" I had moments of joy and peace to be sure, but overall, I was discouraged and confused.

Upon being told after my fourth miscarriage that "everything happens for a reason," I was speechless. This phrase is one I myself have said, but when held up against my many miscarriages, it felt like a slap on the face. "Really?!" I wanted to say in my snarkiest of tones. "So that's how it works—thank you for explaining all of life's great mysteries to me." But instead, I swallowed back my words. Keeping quiet and feeling the tightness moving quickly from my belly to my throat, I held my breath and wondered for the reason. *Why, God? Why?*

In most all of these painful experiences, I said nothing, swallowing back my words, quietly obliging others theirs.

Miscarriage after miscarriage, I slowly began to see the pattern of what gave these comments power over me: the power to hurt. Underneath all of them was the very same message I had been telling myself about my grief and loss from the start, a lie that went something like this: It is not okay for me to be honest about my pain, present to what is, right here where I am. I feared doing so would make me appear weak, faithless, and unworthy.

In time, I began to see things differently. I found it was in loving and accepting my weaknesses, limitations, and flaws that I made the greatest difference for myself and others. It was in sharing my darkest moments that my light shined the brightest. When people said and did things that hurt, instead of feigning indifference, I began to see this other option. I could be honest with them. Instead of suffering in silence, which admittedly felt safer, I realized I could be vulnerable. From somewhere deep inside myself came the permission to be flawed, and from this tolerant, flawed place, instead of hiding my hurting heart, I could admit it.

As I made space in my life to regularly honor, talk about, and remember my angels with the ones I loved, I experienced myself holding up high my own experiences of loss without apology or fear of judgment. I loved all nine of my children, and I always will. Living this sentiment "out loud" in my interactions was empowering, healing, and validating. I began to see the ones who had said or done hurtful things in the past in a new light. The truth was, many people had no clue what I wanted or needed from them, and if I wanted that to change, the power laid within me. I didn't have to be quiet or hide my pain. If I never risked sharing, how would the other person know, and perhaps more importantly, how would I grow?

Another realization I had was that many people just did not know what to do or say. This came into sharp focus for me through an e-mail I received from a friend. The e-mail read, "My friend lost her baby last night. She was 27 weeks pregnant. I don't know what I need to do. I was going to mail her a card tomorrow, but I don't want to do something wrong. What can I do for her?"

Her words said it all. She hurt for her friend, but at the very same time, she felt inadequate to support her because she herself had never experienced the loss of a child. She was scared of doing or saying the wrong thing, worried that even sending a card might offend. But she loved her friend and longed to support her just the same. Tears streamed down my face as I thought of all the many people who likely felt a similar sort of helplessness in supporting me in my losses. How many of my friends and family, worried they might offend, held their tongues? How many that had meant to say the very right thing to comfort me had, instead, said the very "wrong" things?

I sat a minute before replying to my friend. What were the things people said or did that helped me the most? What were the things I wished I'd known to ask for? How could I be there for others, especially other mothers, who knew the pain and loneliness of losing a child either before or after birth?

I sat there a long while, thinking back over all the many years since my first loss in 2005 and all the many things people said and did for me — and a few things I wished they had—and I created my loss to-do list, e-mailing it to my friend. I thanked her for asking and said that though her friend's list may be different, it is always okay to ask. Indeed, the asking alone might be for her friend a very healing thing.

It had been for me.

My Loss To-Do List:

- Listen. Just listen and allow for my grief. This is the most powerful thing you can do.

- Tell me you are sorry.

- Tell me you are thinking of me.

- Tell me you are praying for me, and then do, every night if you can.

- Send me something small to remind me how much you care, or simply call to see how I am doing.

- Hug me. Even when I tell you I'm okay, hug me anyway.

- Say my baby's name. I love to hear it.

- Put this date on your calendar, and remember my angel with me, year after year.

- Give me the gift of you. Your heart. Your tears. Your understanding. Your love. Your permission to grieve.

That night, as I thought about how my friend might best love and support her friend, I came home to not only the many ways I wanted to be loved, but the ways I can be there for others.

What things belong on your loss to-do list?

xoxo,
Suzanne

"People told me that God didn't want me to parent Rocco. Some said, 'Don't cry. Be strong for your kids and be grateful that at least you have them.' The worst one was, 'Well, how can you really miss him when you didn't know him?'"

—AnnMarie Gubenko

Survival Tip #6: Believe that you have the right to your feelings, no matter how small your baby was. *Your loss counts.*

She Was Real

By Kelly DeBie

I firmly believe that we become mothers in our hearts the moment that we first begin to think that we might be pregnant. We are sometimes attached to the idea of our children long before their existence can even be confirmed by medical science.

With that attachment comes all the bonding, the planning, the dreams of the future that accompany motherhood. Within milliseconds we are imagining what they will look like, what they will love, who they will grow up to be.

Sadly, not all those babies get to grow up. Some of them don't make it to their first birthday. Some of them never make it home from the hospital. Some of them never even make it into our arms.

My first child was one of them.

She was real, and her name was Hannah.

I can honestly say that the time she was a part of my life included some of the happiest moments I have ever been lucky enough to experience. She came to be much earlier than we had ever intended to have children because my husband was diagnosed with cancer shortly after we were married. When you are young and have your entire life ahead of you, and someone tells you that you might never be able to have children naturally after cancer treatment and gives you a few weeks to bank sperm, you suddenly want them more than anything else in the world.

Though we had a very narrow window of opportunity to try, we tried.

It worked.

On the day that my husband finished radiation, we discovered that I was pregnant. It seemed as if our lives had been completely derailed by cancer and all our priorities had been shifted for a reason.

She was the light at the end of that tunnel.

We shouted our news from the rooftops. Our joy could not be contained, it seemed, and everyone around us rejoiced with us. We'd ridden the roller coaster for months by then, going from a young, healthy couple, to a cancer patient and his wife, to a potentially infertile couple, to parents.

That joy disappeared one afternoon in a dimly lit ultrasound room when the technician quietly slipped out the door and a doctor came in to deliver the news that the heart had stopped beating. The baby was dead.

The following days were a blur, and in those moments I realized a lot about how poorly equipped our medical system truly is to help mothers who have lost their children.

I was too far along at 12 weeks to wait it out. The baby had been dead for some time, yet my body hadn't begun to expel it alone. I was left with no choice but some kind of intervention. They recommended a D & C, though they informed me that the procedure would have to take place in the women's hospital and my recovery would be on the same floor with new mothers and their infants. That held no appeal to me, and the absolute last place I wanted to be in the world was anywhere near a labor and delivery unit.

I was offered an in-office procedure, which they insisted was safe. I didn't have it in me at the time to ask many questions, so I just agreed. The following day, I sat alone in the waiting room for what seemed like forever, surrounded by pregnant women and their children.

The nurse still insisted on weighing me and demanded that I give a urine sample, even though the tears were streaming down my face.

The dilating medication was placed directly on my cervix, and she took my hand to help me sit up. Then she informed me that it was going to hurt and that I may want to stop and pick up a heating pad. She gave me a list of things I needed to go to the emergency room for and wished me good luck. Good luck?

After hours of excruciating contractions at home, the baby was gone just after midnight on January 15, 2000. I spent most of the day curled up in the fetal position.

I know in my heart that she was a girl. Her name was Hannah. She was real.

People said things, lots of things, with the intention to be helpful. They said things like the following:

- "You are young."
- "Maybe someday you can have more babies."
- "Maybe it was the cancer."
- "God has a plan."
- "It's for the best."
- "It was better to lose the baby now."
- "At least she wasn't born with problems."
- "Heaven has another angel."
- "I'm sure there was something wrong, and that's why."
- "Now you can finish school."
- "It's just a miscarriage."

None of them helped. Nothing anyone said made me feel better. Most of it made me cry. Some made me angry. Some made me ask questions that couldn't be answered. Most made me question my faith. It didn't matter that people had good intentions. They didn't help. I just wanted to cry and be left alone.

I just wanted people to acknowledge her. I wanted people to tell me that my grief was okay. I wanted them to know that I was lost, a childless mother, going through the motions. I wanted them to know that I saw everything differently now, and that while things had continued on just as they always had for each of them, my life would never be the same again.

I wanted people to understand that even if she wasn't real to them, that even if I never got to hold her in my arms, that even if I never had a single picture of her, and that even if I never could smell her skin and count her toes and feel her warmth against my chest, *she was real to me.*

She was, and will forever be, my first child, even if no one else understands.

She made me a mother, and just because she died didn't invalidate that. Without her, I wouldn't be who I am now. I wouldn't have the children I have now. I wouldn't be this person.

She changed me. Forever.

After I lost her, I felt like my life was rapidly spinning out of control. I was in school at the time, but had already taken a leave in part because of my husband's illness. Many days, I just couldn't go. Instead I would find myself crying in a parking lot somewhere on some days, or staring at the ocean on others.

I hated that we had told everyone I was expecting. I hated that they all looked at me with sad eyes and didn't know what to say or do around me. I hated it all.

A girl in my class was a few weeks further along than I should have been. I couldn't bear to be anywhere around her. So I stopped going to that class.

Soon, it seemed as if every woman in the world was either pregnant or carrying a newborn. Everyone but me.

At some point, I found myself wandering the mall instead of sitting in a lecture hall, where I was supposed to be. I ended up in a jewelry store and walked immediately to the birthstones. I walked out with a peridot pendant, the birthstone she would have had. I promised myself that I would wear it every day until the day she was supposed to be born, and after that day passed, I would take it off and try to move on.

I know that it sounds silly and superficial, but that necklace helped. I still felt a little bit like I was carrying her with me. I still wear it every year on the day I said good-bye. The rest of the year belongs to the rest of the things in my life, but that day will forever be hers.

After nearly a year of trying, we were told that the radiation had left him sterile and that we would not be able to have children without help. We were told to be grateful that we had banked sperm.

It all made me mourn her even more.

They were wrong. I was already pregnant. I would go on to have four children, the children still with me now. I am so grateful for the chance to be their mother, but I was a mother long before they came.

I had another child.

She was real.

Her name was Hannah.

xoxo,

Kelly D.

"Before I had children, I would think miscarriage was not a big deal. 'But a stillborn—that's a big deal.' I was young and didn't know a thing. But the minute I got pregnant, I knew that was not true."

—Jennie Goutet

Your Loss Counts

By Katia Bishops

How do you write about a miscarriage at 8 weeks and explain the magnitude of your loss amidst heartbreaking stories of multiple miscarriages, infant loss, and infertility? Or protect the memory of the event from trivialization when you feel as though you've already failed once before at rescuing that promise of a child from "words of comfort" that erased him (and yes, you knew it was a "he"), best intentioned words that you would use yourself — *have* used yourself — before you knew, with words like, "it was not a person yet," and "thank goodness it happened so early"?

Words from those closest to you, desperately trying to walk in your shoes. Words of the non-initiated into this kind of loss. How do you talk about being broken when you already have one child who's your entire world, the best child on the planet? How do you talk about that to the non-initiated into parenthood without sounding greedy?

You could try and start with loss and talk about the fact that this wasn't the first time you've lost him, it was just the most painful one. You've been losing him almost every month for an entire year. Every time the fertility clinic called to deliver another no.

After that, perhaps you'll want to move on to history. The milestones and significant moments that make a relationship. Yours won't consist of the first time he smiled at you, or the first time he said "Mama," but you have a history, nonetheless. One that did not stop being just because your baby did. That tiny voice speaks to you through everyday objects which despite themselves became symbols of him; two brownish Calvin Klein dresses you bought with your mom the first time you went shopping for your much-too-quickly-expanding waistline. You couldn't wait to wear them. You're pretty sure you ended up wearing one for *that* appointment. Or the calming loose leaf lavender tea you were drinking to un-break yourself? The Collingwood vacation photos? All him! He was not quite there yet, but his presence is more palpable and concrete than any of the other family members' smiling images. He's hovering, the promise of him about to become reality a mere week later, but the "you" in the picture doesn't know it yet.

Any of it. You are still broken and not yet broken at the same time. Those family photos? Forever him.

You may want to finish by addressing that "greediness." You remember a caring friend struggling to find words of comfort and finally deciding on: "At least you're already blessed with one child." You remember swallowing through a lump in your throat and nodding. You *remember once thinking the exact same thing when contemplating somebody else's loss.* This was your eye-opener. No, you're not being greedy or ungrateful. Yes, you already have a wonderful child, who fills you up completely. He is the precise reason you need another one. You want more than anything in the world to give back to that child.

When you lose a child in early pregnancy, you will hear a lot of words that won't comfort you — they're usually different variations of the same couple of sentences. You will also hear a few words that will; those will differ from one grieving mom to another. Not knowing you personally, I can't tell which ones will work for you. I wish I could offer words of comfort, but I can't, except for maybe these: it doesn't matter if you were at 8, 18, or 28 weeks. *Your loss counts.*

I remember reaching out to a friend who experienced a loss in the third trimester shortly after my own miscarriage. I wanted her to know I understood, but my tone was apologetic. I was afraid she would think I was equating the earth-shattering magnitude of my loss at 8 weeks with her almost full-term pregnancy loss. She messaged me back, "A loss is a loss."

So many of us feel guilty proclaiming our early pregnancy loss as such — a loss. We worry that the use of the word by us may not be "legitimate" when there is surely somebody else out there who has it worse, sometimes right in front of our eyes.

But you know what? That's just what moms do. They feel guilty. Motherhood and guilt so often go hand in hand. You have a history with your baby, even if he's not there. And you're a mom, even if your baby was never born.

Love,
Katia B.

"I remember more than a few people telling me I was lucky that I lost my first pregnancy at ten weeks, before I got too attached. I know in their own way they were trying to help, but of course we know that that is no help at all. I still remember watching an interview Mary Tyler Moore did, around the time of my losses, so it had to be about sixteen or seventeen years ago. She had lost her son and sister, both in their early twenties, but she was talking about a miscarriage she had, and she said it was the hardest loss she had gone through because it was so lonely and private. That statement made me feel so much more entitled to my grief."

—Kathy Radigan

Perspective Change

By Sandi Haustein

I lay still while the ultrasound tech squirted the warm, gooey gel over my stomach. I had been spotting for three days, and after what I had seen in the bathroom that morning, I was sure that I was miscarrying. Crying all the way to the doctor's office, I had arrived and fallen into my husband's arms. Now, I lay back, gripping my husband's hand, my heart racing, waiting for the evidence of what I already knew to be true.

But right away, my heart was yanked in an unexpected direction as the image of my baby appeared on the screen. The baby was moving — jumping, really — and the tech pointed out a strong heartbeat. My eyes grew wide. My jaw dropped. I looked at my husband in disbelief. The picture of our baby bouncing up and down made my belly shake with tears of joy and relief. I smiled at my husband, and we squeezed each other's hands tighter. We were going to have one of those happy endings, the one you tell your child her whole life. *We thought we were going to lose you, Little One, but God had something bigger planned for you.* For the next thirty minutes, we watched our baby jump and swim, with amazed smiles on our faces and silent tears running down our cheeks.

In that moment, there was no way to know that when my husband returned to work, and I went home alone, the blood would begin to pour. I would be sobbing in my bathroom, begging God to save the little baby that I had just seen alive and well.

There was no way to know that in five hours I'd be sitting in this same chair, with this same ultrasound tech, looking up at the same screen — only this time, there would be no jumping, swimming baby. The screen would be empty.

There was no way to know.

I struggled with many heart-wrenching questions as I replayed the events of my miscarriage over and over in my head. If I had rested when I first started spotting, would my baby have been okay? When I saw her moving on the ultrasound, was she in pain? What happened between seeing her on the ultrasound in the morning and the empty screen in the afternoon? It felt like a cruel joke, that God would let me see my baby alive, only to yank away her life so quickly. I felt deeply hurt and betrayed by Him, who I thought was supposed to love me. Old scabs from childhood losses were torn open; familiar lies crept to the surface of my heart.

You're all alone.

No one cares about your pain.

Others have suffered more and matter more.

Allowing myself to spin downward into negativity, I entered into a deep depression. For four months, I withdrew and isolated myself from my friends, only leaving my house to take my son to preschool or to go grocery shopping or to fake my way through my twice-a-month moms group. I woke up most days in a panic, crying and anxious over nothing in particular. I spent hours lying in bed, escaping into books or just staring, not feeling any purpose to my life. Undirected anger consumed me, and it took all I had not to unleash it on my husband and three sons.

Then, one day, I found the courage to contact a family counselor who specialized in childhood trauma, an important part of my own grief puzzle. Having miscarried herself, she listened to my story with compassion and told me she felt honored that I would trust her with my pain. She listened to my other stories of loss as well, and one day, after a particularly emotional story, she told me that she felt as if God wanted me to know that He sees me. God sees me? Scenes from my life flashed before me, like a movie reel, beginning and ending with that afternoon in my bathroom when I was sobbing, bleeding, and begging. Until that moment, I never realized how unseen I had felt.

He sees me.

Realizing that God was there with me in that bathroom, seeing me in the most intimate, vulnerable moment of my life, made me feel cared for and loved. I pictured Him stroking my hair, His heart broken by my tears. I pictured Him looking at me with eyes of love, knowing that one day, I'd look back and realize that He'd been there at that sacred moment when my baby passed from one life to the other. Once my eyes were opened, I began to see lots of ways that God had tried to show His love to me. Even those thirty minutes in that ultrasound room became a beautiful gift instead of a cruel joke. Watching our little one jump on that screen gave me hope and celebration in the middle of an awful, traumatic day. Those thirty sacred minutes were frozen in time, and no one could take them away from me.

My journey out of depression wasn't an easy one, but once I began to take steps forward, I was able to allow more and more healthy things into my life. My doctor prescribed antidepressants for me that allowed me to process my grief with a clearer mind. I continued counseling. I began sharing my miscarriage story with safe friends. I started an online healthy habits competition with some friends to help me fit in the exercise that I knew would help me feel better and lose the weight that I had gained during my depression. All of these things worked together to help put me on the road to healing.

For Christmas, my husband gave me a beautiful ring to represent our baby, and two years later, I still wear it every day. It's a simple silver band with one word engraved on it: "Hope." Somehow, wearing this ring on my finger gives me something tangible to say that my baby's life mattered, that she meant something to me, to us. I look at that word, Hope, several times a day, re-centering the letters when the ring gets turned, reminding myself that I need re-centering, too, when I start to lose hope for the future. Because one day, when I reach that sacred moment where I pass from one life to the other, God will be waiting for me, holding hands with a little child who's waiting to meet her mother.

I can't wait to hear that heartbeat again.

Sincerely,

Sandi H.

"Fifteen weeks is further than I got with either of mine...
One of the feelings I hate, which makes it all so much
worse, is never feeling absolutely certain that they did
count. I mean, I know intellectually that a moment past
conception, what you have is a human life in its earliest
form, but I barely had the chance to realize they were
there. I mean, I hoped, but I put off testing so as not to
jinx it, and then the confirmation for both came in losing
them.

And they totally feel like non-events, yet the most
traumatic non-events ever, which have changed me
drastically."

—Lizzi Rogers

Survival Tip #7: Watch for simple, unexpected things that may help you feel better.

It's so important to note that not everything people did after a loss was terrible. We certainly do not want to leave the impression that as you go through your grieving process, people are going to be horrendous to you. We do want to validate your feelings, let you know that you are not the only one who hears hurtful statements, and also educate any friends and family who may decide to read this book.

But this is a book of encouragement, and we'd like to share these wonderful things that were done for us after our losses.

Kelly P: An office friend of mine asked if she could hang Henry's picture on her bulletin board. That touched me so much. I am friends with her on Facebook and told her that I still remember it six years later. She has since moved, changed jobs, and had a son of her own. She shared with me that she still has his picture on her bulletin board and a note I wrote her that she keeps in her office drawer. She said they remind her to keep things in perspective when she's having a bad day.

Anna D: On Jack's birthday, my neighbors lined our driveway with luminarias. The candles glowed as we pulled in after a hard, emotional day, and each paper bag had a note written on it with a special memory of Jack, written by one of Jack's friends or teachers.

Sarah B: Nicest thing someone did for me: For several weeks after my miscarriage, my little sister called me every single night to talk. Sometimes we talked about the miscarriage; sometimes it was just about our day. She didn't know what I was going through, but she wasn't afraid to reach out to me every day to see how I was doing. I will always treasure that.

Alexa B: I had several friends and family members who brought me mementos with Kathryn's name on them. One friend bought me a beautiful little necklace pendant that has tiny footprints on the front and Kathryn's initials and birth date on the back. Another friend sent me a simple Christmas ornament with Kathryn's name on it. We have been given keepsakes and other treasures. My aunt blew me away by sending me a stack of beautiful laminated cards with all of Kathryn's information on the front of the card, and the poem "Little Angels" on the back. These cards were for me to give to anyone I wanted to. Every time I see the card on my fridge, I feel my spirits lifted. Additionally, the nurse in the NICU who cared for Kathryn the night she passed sent me a card about six months later. She just simply stated that she thought of us often and prayed for us daily. Her kind gesture truly warmed my heart.

AnnMarie G: My neighbors took turns making dinners for us for two months. It really helped me a lot.

Lizzi R: My mum and aunty bought me an original painting of an orchard in bloom as a kind of memorial, so I could write the name and date of loss on the back. That was very sweet. And my best friend made sure she bought me a Mother's Day card this year. That was nice but made me cry a lot (partly because it was the day after my second loss, and I'd not told her at that point).

Heather W: The ladies in my due-date group joined together and sent me a beautiful sterling silver necklace with Clara's name, birth date, and birthstone. They also sent dozens of cards and gift cards for our family. It was the most beautiful gesture, and I wear that necklace every single day.

Sandi H: I have several things:

One of my closest friends bought me a plant that has "angel" in the title. I have never been able to keep a plant alive, but this one sits in my kitchen windowsill, and my husband and I take turns watering it. Two years later, it is a sweet reminder of my little one. After my second miscarriage, the same friend was planting trees in her yard and had my youngest son pick one of them as "our" tree in memory of the second baby.

Three weeks after my first miscarriage, I was at a family reunion where most everyone knew about my loss, but no one was saying anything about it. When I saw one of my oldest cousins for the first time, she hugged me, looked straight in my eyes, and said, "I'm so sorry for your loss. Your heart must feel full and empty all at the same time." It meant so much to me.

My first miscarriage was in August 2011. That next March was my due date, and of course, I was dreading that week and not knowing if anyone else remembered. I got a message on Facebook from a girl that I knew in college, not very well, but she wrote, "Sandi, you were on my heart today. I'm sitting here nursing my four-day-old baby girl, my first. I remember that you and Dave have a sweet baby in heaven that would be born about the same time as ours. I want you to know that I'm praying for you and I have a vivid picture of what your sweet baby is like from getting to know mine, and I know you will be able to love on her or him in heaven someday. I'm sure you are a wonderful momma already, and I pray God's blessings on you and your family. Love you." I know that this could have been hurtful to some, but at that moment, it was beautiful to me that a first-time mom would at all be thinking of someone who'd lost a baby with a similar due date. She acknowledged my little one, and she remembered.

Kristi B: A friend wrote an acrostic poem for me using Naomi's name. Also, we asked people to donate to a crisis pregnancy center in our baby's name, and that meant a lot to us.

Regina P: One of the midwives in the practice I went to offered to do a drawing of a picture of William (preemie photos are very raw and harsh). When she sent the drawing and photo back to me, the package included an oil painting that her *mother* had done, along with a note that said her mother was so moved by our story that she wanted to help. This drawing and painting are two of my most prized possessions, to this very day!

"It's okay to have happy days, too.
Don't feel guilty about laughing or
having fun with your other loved ones.
Some of our biggest laughs and widest
smiles come from talking about Joey and
the crazy things he did. Finding peace
and happiness is part of healing, too."

—Kathy Glow

Chapter 4: You Are Not a Failure

You are not a failure or less of a woman if you have miscarried multiple times or are never able to carry a pregnancy to term. 1 in 4 pregnancies end in miscarriage. Sadly, You are not alone. And more importantly, you are not a failure.

Survival Tip #8: Know that infertility is a bitch. Sometimes you get a happy ending, and sometimes you have to pursue a different happy ending.

Welcome to the Invisible Mom's Club

By Lizzi Rogers

I'm sorry to say that when I joined the Invisible Mom's Club, there was no pleasant welcome.

No tables of drinks and nibbles were laid out. No other members were milling around, waiting to welcome me with open arms into their ranks. In fact, I'd go so far as to say that taking out membership was one of the most profoundly painful and lonely moments of my life — *at first.*

My husband and I had given ourselves some time after getting married in 2010. Time to get used to the idea of living together and make it work for *us*. Time alone before embarking upon the journey of Having A Family. We were widely endorsed, largely by people with children, and we felt that with their "insider knowledge," this was probably a very good idea, after all. We wouldn't want to squander the only precious time we might have alone for the next twenty years or so, would we?

With clear consciences and a certain smugness at the rightness of our decision, I began taking birth control pills once we were married, and we rejoiced in the simplicity of modern medicine which not only would allow us to pick the "perfect" time for us to have our first child, but would also prevent me from ovulating, so there was no chance we might accidentally conceive and then lose any potential children—which was *not* something we were prepared to contemplate. We wanted our children alive, intact, and when we were good and ready.

The first two years of marriage were hard on us. We were in a tiny flat and my husband's health deteriorated (he'd previously been diagnosed with type 1 diabetes), resulting in him losing his PhD position at our city's university. In the meantime, I'd gone back to college to study a frivolous qualification because I'd thought it would be okay. So there we were, one student and one signed off sick, and neither of us in a fit state to bring a child into the world. We clung to the idea that we'd done the right thing with regard to not having children, and congratulated ourselves on our foresight.

Until August 2012, when we received some devastating news.

The extent of my husband's condition was finally diagnosed after a couple of years of relentless testing. His hypothalamus was broken, which meant (essentially) his endocrine system had shut down. He was running on less than empty. The treatment to get him back to a sufficient state of health for day-to-day life was testosterone — which, once taken, would render him permanently infertile.

We panicked. We pleaded. I cried. Not now! Not so soon! We haven't even begun our family yet!

We were granted a reprieve of less than a year of alternative treatment, which would aim to improve his (already failing) fertility and allow us time to conceive.

So we got down to business.

In the last days of October, something was different. I felt changes in my body that I'd never felt before. My boobs hurt, and I was peeing like a racehorse every five minutes. I stayed away from Google, but my husband looked up symptoms of early pregnancy, and we clasped those affirmations to our hearts in glee. I was determined not to test yet, as Aunt Flo (AF) was due a week later.

A really long week later. And she was late.

She was late all week, and I decided that I'd take the test on the final day I'd expected her to be here, just to indulge in the deliciousness of the truth in an absolutely undeniable way.

I waited with bated breath for Friday to come, and when it did, I got up early and managed to make a complete mess of the test in my excitement.

It was negative.

I was absolutely stunned. I still had symptoms, hadn't I? I still felt weird. I was still very late for AF.

I spent the day feeling very lacklustre and slightly terrified. I told myself I'd test again in the morning. Perhaps I just hadn't given it enough time or I was one of those women whose hormone levels remained naturally low. Perhaps, perhaps...

That night the cramping started. Unusually vicious cramping.

Followed by spotting.

Followed by lots and lots and lots of blood. And lumps. And clots. And absolutely the worst feeling in the world, as I knew by then, that what I was disposing of so casually was my first child.

I felt hollow.

I tried so hard to carry on with my daily life, to ignore the vicious increase in pain and gore. To pretend that it was okay, after all, and that this happens to lots of women. Especially on their first pregnancy. And it was such an early pregnancy, it barely counted, did it? Besides, my family has a history of struggling to carry boys; this could almost have been expected.

With each visit to the bathroom, I felt more and more at a loss.

I've always believed what science proves: at conception, what is present is a human life in its earliest form. And here I was, not commemorating that life, not respecting it, but pouring it secretly into the sewers from a variety of locations. Not just any life, either, but the life of my child, who I (as its mother) was supposed to have been able to nourish, grow, nurture, and respect.

I was absolutely wretched.

My husband and I grew distanced. He didn't understand what it was like, and in the ensuing months, when my mood would dip as AF turned up, or when I pulled away from him in bed because, well, that's what had led to us losing our child, I had to explain over and over how terrible I felt. How alone. How in pain.

But there was one tiny upshot.

The Invisible Mom's Club.

When I first announced my miscarriage (a terrible thing to have to do, by all accounts, but an announcement I was determined to make so that I didn't have to explain my lack of competence/involvement/capability at the time), women began coming out of the woodwork with their stories of loss.

Soon I realised that I was absolutely surrounded—by family, friends, acquaintances, strangers—and I began making connections.

We were all members. Yet somehow (probably because it's not yet an appropriate topic for the dinner table), I'd never known. The taboos were in force, and I'd never seen behind the barriers to this club.

Each woman who opened up to me showed me a glimpse of her pain. And in sharing that pain with me, helped to shoulder my own burden of hurt. I'd known that the statistics for miscarriage were high; I'd even known a couple of people who'd gone through one, but never, until now, had I known so viscerally that the invisible moms were *everywhere*.

But here's the thing: they often expressed the feelings of isolation that I had felt.

We were all alone, together.

It seems so ridiculous that in a modern, enlightened society, *any* woman should need to feel as though she's entering this club alone, unsupported, with no one to hold her hand. Because joining it is terrible. But feeling alone in the room is far worse.

So I began writing and soapboxing, and using my blog as a platform to combat the taboos surrounding miscarriage. I felt I was honouring my Neverborn by striving to ensure that there was a real account out there — a resource which might be accessed by women just beginning their membership, so that they might find some solidarity.

Then, in March 2013, AF was late again. I resolved not to test at the end of one week, because last time it had brought such heartache. I decided to wait for a fortnight and test on a Monday morning before I left for college. The second week was passing, and I allowed my gaze to linger on the box of pregnancy tests each time I passed them by. Excitement was building. Maybe this time…?

On Saturday, the bleeding started.

On Sunday it was Mother's Day, and I sat in church, silent, grieving, numb.

A little kid came up to me to give me a bunch of flowers and said, "For all the ladies, on Mother's Day." I smiled wanly and hid them in my bag. I didn't want them. I didn't deserve them. Once again,

I'd failed at being a nurturing mother; my second baby was dead within me.

I spent the next few weeks in determined denial of that truth.

I'd previously sought counselling to help cope with the loss of my first, and gradually felt safe enough to explain what had happened that Mother's Day weekend. The counsellor confirmed my worst fears.

"It sounds very much like you had another miscarriage. I'm sorry."

My soul twisted in pain as I realised that I needed to accept and acknowledge this new, cold truth. Two babies lost. Two potential lives I'd never meet or hold or get to know. Two children snuffed out for some reason beyond my ken.

My friends and family rallied around me, and I realised now, more than ever, that I needed them — all of them, including the ones I met and spoke to on a regular basis; those far away with whom I could only talk on the telephone; those I'd grown close to online; and those in support groups I'd joined. They all played their part in gradually hauling me out of that pit of despair.

It was a slow climb though, with many regressions along the way, and those wonderful people (largely women) were there for me every step along the way. They listened to my rants and whines. They encouraged me to take positive action. They supported my writing.

With this double membership to the Invisible Mom's Club, I got to thinking (and writing) hard about my situation. It's a strange place to be, because the members absolutely are mothers, but they have no children to show for the status. There's a case for labelling it a "dual reality," because on the one, hidden side, is the grief and loss, both so very real, for a real person, and on the other, when we go out, there is no sign at all that we are parents.

I found this very difficult to deal with, and I was prone to outbursts of anger and sadness. I couldn't look at a pregnant woman without glaring and wishing she were me. I hid Facebook updates from friends with young babies. I ranted and cried and wished things were different, but once you're part of this club, you're in it for life.

I began to think about trying again (I couldn't get out of my head that sex equalled baby loss, and I went out of my way to avoid intimacy with my husband) when we got an advance on the situation we'd been trying to delay; a sperm count to check the progress of treatment revealed one lonely swimmer. Apparently this is a nearly unheard-of happenstance, and it impressed the laboratory technician sufficiently that she felt called to remark upon it when delivering the news (bear in mind that a "low" sperm count is somewhere in the region of six million swimmers per millilitre).

With the rug pulled from under our feet for a third time, I decided to try a new tack. I sought all the support I could from those wonderful women around me, and began writing in earnest, pouring my heart into developing the resources online for women like me. And I began to get responses and encouragements; people had been touched by my words. I had helped. I had Done Something Real!

As time went by, I made a conscious (and very excruciatingly hard) decision to give up the dream of having biological children in the hopes that someday, we might be able to adopt. I didn't want to bring any build-up of long-nurtured resentment into a relationship which would naturally be so fragile at the start. I want my adopted child to know that they are not a replacement, not a second best, and definitely not a consolation prize. I want them to be purely and simply mine.

In the meantime, as we wait to see whether adoption is a possibility for us, I am committed to writing and sharing my story in as many ways and through as many platforms as possible.

Because I am my children's legacy, and I want to honour them by providing (where possible) that welcoming smile; recognition; that shoulder to cry on to women struggling with the terrible news that made them a member of the Invisible Mom's Club.

If it's you who's just joined (or maybe you've been a member for a while), I hope from the bottom of my heart that you haven't felt isolated or alone. It's a very sad club to be part of, but there is a silver lining. The members are everywhere, and there are places and women you can turn to whenever you need them. They can't fix what's happened or restore your non-membership status (believe me, we'd all love to), but when you find a group of women who are prepared to support you, listen to you, and hold you in their hearts and encourage you as you move forward, you will find that the treasure in that silver lining is rich indeed.

Welcome to the Invisible Mom's Club—let me show you around.

Love,

Lizzi

"I'm totally blurred about what I feel saddest about: Neverborn #1, Neverborn #2, or the subsequent infertility diagnosis, rendering them both bitterly ironic."

—Lizzi Rogers

Please Don't Let Me Have a Fifth Miscarriage

By Kathy Radigan

Well, it's happened. I've finally flipped.

This was the thought that occurred to me after I had spent my whole 45-minute bus ride into work obsessing on the fact that we didn't have enough life insurance on my husband.

The year was 1998. We had recently moved from Manhattan to Queens, so I was now taking a commuter bus in to my job as an assistant in a venture capital firm.

The whole ride in, I kept thinking about the fact that we never bought life insurance for Joe. Why didn't we do that? Shouldn't we have a policy for my husband? Sure, he has one through his job, but that wasn't much money.

For the life of me, I couldn't understand why I was obsessing on this. I had a job, we had no children, and we didn't even own our house. Why would I need extra life insurance on Joe? It was ridiculous, yet I couldn't stop these insidious thoughts. Obviously it was time to take my fertility doctor up on her offer to give me some referrals to a therapist familiar with infertility issues. It finally happened. I had slipped into the abyss of madness.

The previous year and a half, we had endured four miscarriages, fertility tests, genetic testing, and three attempts at assisted reproduction with drugs. We'd had it. We'd decided to get off the baby roller coaster and concentrate on us for a while.

I actually thought I was feeling better. But since I couldn't stop having obsessive thoughts about silly things, I guessed I was worse off than I thought.

As I got closer to my office, I made the decision to take one more pregnancy test. I wasn't even really late. But I knew I would rest easier once I knew I wasn't pregnant.

How could it be possible? We weren't "trying." After the shots, the pills, and the calls from my doctor telling me when we should have sex, it wasn't possible to just get pregnant the good old-fashioned way. Was it? Could I finally be getting my happy ending?

No. I wouldn't allow myself to think that way. I'd been devastated four times before. Our story wouldn't end so neatly; I just wasn't that lucky. I needed to stop torturing myself.

I picked up the familiar pink box and paid for it. I thought, Okay. Once I get the negative test result, I'll call the doctor, get back on the pill, and get the name of a therapist. A really, really good one.

I went right to the ladies' room and took the test by rote. One line and then another line appeared.

I stood in shock.

Pregnant. Again.

My heart was beating fast.

Pure joy and intense dread filled every corner of my body at the same exact time.

I quickly went to my desk and called my doctor. "Come right in. We'll take some blood."

I popped my head into my boss's office. "Mike, I have to run out for a while. I'll be back as soon as possible." Then I hailed a cab. There was a real benefit to working for the same person for seven years. He knew everything we'd been through, so my need to run out of the office wasn't questioned.

In the time it took the cab to drive the twenty blocks to my doctor's office, I'd gone through the possibility that this could finally be the miracle I was praying for. I also realized that I might have to endure a fifth miscarriage. A fifth miscarriage. How could I possibly endure that?

My mind went back in time to my first miscarriage. Back then, I couldn't believe how smoothly our road to parenthood was starting out. We got pregnant our first month of trying. That was almost unheard of in my circle of friends. At thirty, I was the youngest in my group. Most of my friends got pregnant only after spending huge amounts of money on specialists or having sex in positions only found in the *Kama Sutra.*

Yet there it was, a positive pregnancy test staring me in the face. Joe and I were beyond thrilled. I told everyone I knew, from family and friends to the guys at the deli where I bought my lunch. I was having a baby. I read pregnancy books faithfully, bought bigger clothes to fit my expanding waistline, and called my husband with urgent requests from the baby, not me, to bring home Häagen Dazs. Each day felt like Christmas.

Ten weeks later, my husband and I excitedly looked at the ultrasound to see our baby.

But there was no heartbeat. We were devastated.

I put all the "Congratulations, You're Expecting" cards in a box, along with the letter from my insurance company informing me that I was now preregistered for my hospital stay for the delivery of our baby on or around May 30.

We prayed and grieved.

A few months later, I was just starting to feel a little bit better when I had the joy of seeing another positive pregnancy test. Surely this would be the one that would take.

Two weeks later, more crying, more praying, more grieving. We repeated this cycle two more times. I was beyond broken.

To make matters worse, we had moved out of the city and into a house in Queens. Babies and kids were everywhere. I started to dread talking to my married friends because I didn't want to hear any more happy announcements of new babies. Pregnant women were everywhere I looked — happy women with big bellies. I hated them.

Our doctor felt we should start thinking about more aggressive drugs and treatments. IVF was suggested. We didn't know what to do next.

Desperate, I decided to go on a prayer vigil. Mind you, though I'm a spiritual person, I'm not very religious in the conventional sense. I felt the need for guidance and took solace in sitting in a church for a few minutes each day. After the thirty days were over, I felt more peaceful. I wasn't pregnant, but I felt ready to move on. We started to think about adoption. I started to exercise, lost 10 pounds, and thought about dyeing my hair blonde. Maybe we would turn the room we painted baby blue into a guest room/office?

But now here I was, in the back of a cab, holding my fifth positive pregnancy test. My fifth positive pregnancy test. I couldn't believe this was happening to me again.

I walked into the doctor's office, waving the white stick.

"That sure is a positive test," said my favorite nurse, beaming.

My doctor popped her head in the office where I was having my blood taken. She smiled as she said they would call me as soon as they got my blood levels.

Once I got back to my office, I was going crazy because I couldn't get in touch with Joe. I sat at my desk, and told no one about what was going on—no easy feat for a chatterbox like me.

Then I got the call.

"Yes, you are pregnant. The levels look great. The doctor wants to see you in a week, and of course call if you need us."

I hung up the phone and was still in a state of shock. I was thrilled out of my mind.

I tried Joe one more time. He answered.

"I just went to see the doctor."

"Oh. Is everything okay? Are you all right?"

"Yeah, I'm fine. Everything…is really great."

Joe started to laugh. He knew. We were both scared but beyond happy. One week away from our fifth wedding anniversary, this was the best gift we could possibly get.

We said "I love you" and hung up.

A week later, I found myself curled up on the bed in the beautiful hotel room we had booked for the weekend to celebrate our anniversary. We had a great time at the restaurant, Windows on the World, on top of the World Trade Center the night before. We were so happy. Visions of babies danced in my head once more.

But now it was morning, and I was doubled over in excruciating pain. How could this possibly be happening again? I cried.

We ordered room service, trying to maintain some semblance of the romantic getaway we had planned. I looked at the gorgeous roses Joe had given me. I knew it was all too good to be true.

The phone rang. The doctor on call that weekend had called us back. Funny how fast you get a call back when you say you think you are having your fifth miscarriage. We knew there was nothing that could be done this early into the pregnancy, but it felt good to just touch base with someone. Though I had never met this doctor, he was very sweet and gentle with me as he went over my history and symptoms.

"How bad is the bleeding? Are you okay?"

"Actually I haven't started bleeding yet. I'm just in tremendous pain."

There was a pause on the phone. Then the doctor's voice was very gentle.

"Mrs. Radigan, I can't promise you anything, but I don't think you are having a miscarriage."

"No, Doctor, I am. I have been through this four times before. I've never had pain like this."

We both started to laugh. We agreed that maybe that was a good sign. He hung up, telling me to make sure to call my own doctor on Monday and to call him back if anything got worse.

The pain came and went, and it even started to subside through the weekend. We tried to enjoy our getaway, but the thought of what could be happening again was always in our thoughts.

On Monday morning, I was back in my office. As soon as I got to my desk, the phone rang, and it was my doctor's office telling me to come in.

I told Joe I would be fine and would call as soon as I knew anything. I actually wanted to be alone.

Once again I was on the examining table, the familiar sonogram machine in front of me. I told the doctor I wasn't going to look. My favorite nurse held my hand, and we all just waited.

"Kathy…it's okay. You can look." The doctor's voice was very happy.

"It's okay? There's a heartbeat?" I was crying.

"A really great heartbeat."

The nurse and doctor were beaming; I was crying. There on the screen was the heartbeat, the little light blinking, showing me that all was well. I had never seen anything so beautiful in my life.

"Do you want a picture?"

"Yes."

Minutes later, I was back in a cab with my sonogram picture of my little lima bean with the heartbeat. I smiled so hard, my face hurt.

This December, the lima bean from the sonogram celebrates his 15th birthday.

With hope,
Kathy R.

♡

"Sometimes, life is a jumble, and there is just no separating the good from the bad."

—Sheila Quirke

Survival Tip #9: Explore and acknowledge the complicated web of emotions and layers of grief caused by multiple losses.

Examining the Layers of Grief

By Stephanie Sprenger

I have been pregnant five times in my life, and I am fortunate to have two young daughters. However, I have also experienced two early miscarriages and one ectopic pregnancy. Each experience was physically and emotionally painful, and resulted in a wave of complex emotions. My response to the individual losses varied, but I have found that, years later, there is a lingering aftermath brought on by the cumulative losses and their impact on my life. Perhaps the most striking response I had to my pregnancy losses was that there are many layers of grief that go along with early miscarriage, and all of them are valid and need to be explored.

Both of my miscarriages were extremely early, and were considered to be chemical pregnancies; these occur when the fertilized egg never implants, and they usually happen within the first week of a missed period. When I had my ectopic pregnancy, I thought I was having another miscarriage at 5 weeks, but as it turned out, the undetectable egg never went away. Six weeks later, I found out that I was still technically "pregnant." The doctors couldn't find *anything* – not in my uterus and not in my fallopian tube. Having no idea that the pregnancy hadn't dissolved, at 11 weeks I was given an injection of Methotrexate to help break up the pregnancy tissue.

Each time I suffered a loss, I grieved, but the layers of my grief were unique to each experience. My first loss was more notably isolating and stigmatizing than the others; I did not yet realize that miscarriage was somewhat common, and I lacked a support system to help guide me through my complicated web of fears and feelings. In the eight years that followed, I have met many women who have had miscarriages at various stages of pregnancy, and the feeling of community and understanding we have shared played a crucial role in my coping.

During those bewildering days after my first miscarriage, I was engulfed by sorrow, fear, and anger. Though I had less than three days to process my new pregnancy, I had already developed a deep attachment to the idea that I was having a baby. The sadness I felt at the loss of this dream was immense; when one is experiencing a miscarriage, there is no sense of perspective or appreciation of the "big picture." You don't care that you may eventually go on to become pregnant; you could potentially be the mother of four children someday. In that instant, it doesn't matter. You want to be pregnant *right now,* and the idea that you have to wait an unknown amount of time to carry a child is devastating.

The fear I experienced weighed heavily on me; *why* had I miscarried? What was wrong with me? I worried that my body may never be capable of sustaining a pregnancy. The lack of insight into what had gone wrong was overwhelming. I wanted answers; there were none. *These things happen.*

I was surprised to discover a layer of anger to my grief; I felt like I had been cheated; of course, I had promptly purchased the requisite copy of *What To Expect When You're Expecting,* and I had the sensation that I had just been kicked out of The Baby Club. I was embarrassed by my initial enthusiasm, and the tiny white hat I bought for my unborn baby seemed to taunt me, mocking my naïve hopefulness.

The second time I miscarried, I had a four-year-old daughter, and I was extremely cautious about the pregnancy. I waited a few days, had some blood work done that was less than optimistic, and was not surprised when I started to bleed by the end of the week. I was disappointed and sad, but I lacked the fear that I would be unable to conceive again. This time, I had the history to comfort me; I had been through it before and had a healthy pregnancy, so I felt reasonably confident I would be able to have a second child without difficulty.

The ectopic pregnancy followed shortly on the heels of the second loss. Nobody could tell me precisely what had happened, so I was terrified. The undetectable egg and lack of explanation were too much for my controlling temperament to handle. My sense of confidence that history would repeat itself and I would go on to quickly conceive was turned on its head. I was disoriented, shaken, and frightened.

When one loses a pregnancy, the most obvious loss is that of a baby. The grief that presents itself at the forefront is clearly the sorrow over the loss of a baby that will never be born; the dreams of the family you had envisioned. In those weeks and months after my losses, I spent a lot of time reflecting on the myriad of emotions bombarding me, and I realized that there were several other layers to my grief that needed to be explored.

With each of these losses, and perhaps more accurately with the sum of all three, *I felt that I lost confidence in my body.* I felt defective. I wanted to believe that my body, perfectly designed to conceive and carry babies, was fully capable of this biological task. To discover that *your* body didn't get the memo on how to get or stay pregnant is beyond disheartening. It is humiliating. It is scary. For me, my pregnancy losses encapsulated my belief that I could not trust my body.

In addition to losing trust in my body's ability to reproduce, I also lost my pregnancy innocence in many ways. After that first miscarriage, each conception was approached somewhat gingerly rather than joyfully. Should my husband and I someday decide to have a third child, the moment my pregnancy test turns pink, the initial flush of excitement will be immediately followed by a grim resignation to the unknown. I was never able to, nor will I ever again be able to, receive the news of a pregnancy with complete optimism and confidence; the process of conception will never be carefree for me. Although nobody is given any guarantees with pregnancy, until you have experienced a pregnancy loss, it is difficult to grasp the sense of dread and the attempt to prepare yourself for disappointment that is mixed in with the excitement of a new pregnancy.

I felt almost foolish for being preoccupied with my grief about the perception of my body's inadequacy and the disappointment of losing my innocence. Did these things really matter when the most important loss was that of a baby? At first I chastised myself for my feelings of disillusionment, but ultimately I realized that the only way to deal with my emotions was to give voice to *all* of them — even the ones that made me feel ashamed.

There were many things that helped me cope with these complicated layers of grief, but I think giving myself permission to express these dark emotions was the most important. I wanted to stamp my feet and shout, "I just want to have an exciting, easy pregnancy! I feel ripped off that I will never be able to trust my body! Why can't I be one of the women who got pregnant without any complications?" I needed to say these things, to write them down, admit them to myself, talk about them with other women who had experienced it. It made me feel less small to acknowledge the frightened, angry part of myself and receive validation from those who understood.

The last thing a woman who has lost a pregnancy or child should ever do is be ashamed of her emotional reaction. *Accepting your feelings — all of them — is an important key to healing.* I found that I had feelings of anger and resentment when I was around other pregnant women; I couldn't contain my own bitterness when I saw a woman who was pregnant or had an infant. I felt very guilty about my emotional reaction, but ultimately I gave myself permission to honor my own experience, and I kept myself as sheltered as possible from being around pregnancy and babies until I felt less raw.

I was fortunate to have a companion during my second miscarriage; an acquaintance and I had shyly announced our early pregnancies at the baby shower of a mutual friend; sadly we lost them both within days of each other. Our shared circumstances brought us closer together, and I found that she was the only person I wanted to talk to during those challenging weeks. I didn't want to hear comforting words from anyone else; it was essential to me that someone could truly empathize with me *right at that moment,* and that she wouldn't judge me for wallowing, complaining, sobbing, or lashing out. If you do not have a person in your life that can relate to your loss, find someone. There are many online groups for other mothers who have lost a baby or a pregnancy, and often those connections are the ones that bring you closer to healing.

In addition to accepting and expressing my feelings, it was crucial that I shielded myself from allowing others to share well-intentioned advice and wisdom. There are some phrases that are intended to be comforting to people who are grieving that can either fall flat or be perceived as offensive. I did not want to hear anyone tell me, "If it's meant to be, it's meant to be," or "God has a plan," or "There must have been something wrong with this baby." I was well aware that people were trying to help me, and it is difficult to know what to say to a woman who has miscarried, but I still did not want to listen to these sentiments. I also found that I couldn't bear to have people look at me as though they felt sorry for me. **I was painfully aware of the contradictory nature of my needs; on the one hand, I wanted empathy, but I also felt compelled to shout, "Don't you dare feel sorry for me!"** As uncomfortable as I was by feelings that seemed irrational to me, I tried to stop judging myself and accept that my needs often changed from minute to minute. I allowed myself to build a cocoon until I was stronger, and that was one of the best things I did for myself.

Honoring my own authentic beliefs and feelings, giving myself permission to fully grieve over every aspect of my loss, protecting myself from potentially hurtful comments from outsiders, and finding another mother to grieve with were all instrumental in my healing. But nothing else was more powerful in helping me move through my pain than giving birth to my daughters. Their presence in my life finally helped me to shed some of the sadness, anger, and fear I had been carrying. I was even able to let go of my belief that my body was inadequate, thanks to the redemptive experience of giving birth to my second daughter.

I was very ill throughout my pregnancy, and the doctors wanted to get the baby out right at my due date. Instead of inducing my labor with drugs, they broke my water and allowed me to wait and see if my body would take over. I wanted to try to make it through as much of my labor as possible without pain medication, though I was not closed off to the possibility of getting an epidural at some point should I need it. When I gave birth to my first child, my labor was medically induced, I received an epidural before my contractions started, and my twelve-hour labor was uncomplicated yet tedious. With my second delivery, I wanted to test the limits of this body that I felt I could not fully trust. I wanted to see exactly what it was capable of.

After four-and-a-half hours of contractions without drugs, my body began to push the baby out; it did so without my conscious authority, as I was standing in the bathroom when I felt the urge to push. My body, wise and intelligent beyond my comprehension, had taken the wheel. I began to panic when the overpowering contractions and need to push came over me; my doula repeated over and over, "Your body was made to do this. Your body was made to do this." Fifteen minutes later, my healthy, seven-pound daughter came into the world. I was flooded with emotion and euphoria as the realization hit me: my body did something right.

I'd like to say that I found a place within me during those blackest of months to gain the perspective that someday everything would be okay. But the truth is, I merely survived it. The perspective came later, when I no longer realized I was looking for it. It takes time to get through that tunnel. Don't rush yourself; allow yourself to be right where you are, honor the full spectrum of your feelings, and surround yourself only with those who build you up and protect you. Build yourself a cocoon for as long as you like, and be assured, when it is time to come out of it, you will emerge.

Hugs,
Stephanie

"The hardest things to hear for me have always been from those who were dismissive of my miscarriage—e.g., 'It was early,' 'There was something wrong,' 'You should be glad it wasn't later,' etc. It was all like pouring salt on an open wound...so eventually I stopped telling people about her. It hurt too much. This is why it's so isolating. I have hope in my heart that this book will help others understand that they are never as alone as they feel. We all get it."

—Kelly DeBie

Chapter 5: Perspectives on Faith or Spirituality through Loss

There are many different perspectives on spirituality and beliefs, and we wanted to share some of our experiences. During a crisis, religion is especially magnified. People will say they are praying for you or tell you they are certain your "angel" in heaven. But as one of our contributors, Sarah B, points out, not everyone believes in angels, may not be comforted by these thoughts and words.

Religion and spiritual journeys differ greatly for grieving parents. Some people turn away from God and some people grow closer, while others question what they have always held to be true. Others have no spiritual journey at all. In my own experience, I weaved in and out of anger, faith, acceptance, disbelief, disappointment, and eventually back to a growing and stronger faith. I still believe that the quiet calmness I experienced while hospitalized, waiting to deliver the babies, was due largely to the fact that we had an army of people, of different faiths and religions, praying for us. As we, the contributors, discussed how to handle this chapter, we decided it was important to make all grieving mothers feel welcome in the discussion. Our contributions include the viewpoints of Christianity, Buddhism, Judaism, and nonbelievers. The tie that binds us all together is how much of an impact our loss had on our lives and beliefs.

"We are Jewish, and though the Jewish faith believes in heaven and all of that, I am still coming to terms with my own feelings about this."

—Tova Gold

It's a Wonderful Life: The Dream of Motherhood

By Sarah Rudell Beach

The waitress hurried over to our table upon hearing the squeals and cheers.

"It's either someone getting married, or someone's having a baby! Which is it?" she asked.

"A baby!" we told her. Still glowing, my husband and I had just told my family our news. My parents would soon have their first grandchild. My sister would become an aunt.

I was barely 4 weeks along. But we had been travelling through Tuscany for several days on an amazing family vacation, and suspicion had mounted over why I was abstaining from all the wonderful Chianti. I had just learned the news a few days before, and my husband and I were ready to share our secret. We toasted the newest family member-to-be and talked due dates, maternity leaves, nurseries, and baby names. If it was a girl, she would be Abigail.

Though I was tired and endured morning sickness, we continued our tour of the Italian countryside. My family still looks back on this vacation as the best one we've ever taken. I was filled with the excitement of the momentous new step in my life, beginning a new journey, embraced by the love and support of my family.

And then...

And then.

Just a few weeks later, I was at home, the journey prematurely over, my pregnancy ending in miscarriage.

And I was alone.

Alone because my husband had stayed in Europe for another month for work.

Alone because I hadn't told anyone else that I was pregnant.

Alone because I told myself my loss was so early, it didn't really count.

Alone because when I turned to online support groups, people asked about my "angel baby."

Alone because where other women had memorials to their miscarriages in their online signatures, in the form of graphics of tiny babies with wings, all I had was the clinical phrase "m/c at 7 weeks."

Alone because I was grieving.

But I didn't believe in angels.

I didn't know what I was grieving.

I only had one doctor's appointment with that pregnancy, the one where the ultrasound confirmed what I already knew: the pregnancy would end. The doctor speculated, given what she saw (or, rather, didn't see) on the ultrasound, that it was a blighted ovum.

I had never heard that term before, so of course I Googled it when I got home. It meant there had never even been an embryo. Conception had occurred, implantation had occurred, and I had been pregnant. But something was genetically wrong, and a baby never even developed.

How could I grieve that?

How could I grieve blood?

*****

My miscarriage was eight years ago, and it is now hard for me to even remember those initial weeks of grief. Not in the sense that I don't *want* to look back on them because it was so painful, but in the sense that I don't really remember what I did.

I do remember a few things. I ate bad food, the food that I had denied myself for the approximately 4 weeks I was pregnant. I read *a lot*. I wanted to learn all I could about blighted ova, miscarriage, and conceiving after miscarriage, as well as the history and genetics and science and old wives' tales, mythology, symbolism, and literary representations of miscarriage. Reading is my most treasured form of self-care, and learning about what had happened, and what was happening to my body and spirit and identity, was a crucial part of how I dealt with my grief and found my way to wholeness again.

And a lot of the readings talked about my angel baby. An angel baby meant nothing to me, as an atheist. The women who assured me in online forums that I had an angel in heaven provided no consolation. Even if I did believe in angels, I asked myself, how could something that was never even a baby become an angel?

Oddly, my doctor's reassurance that there hadn't been a baby, and that I wouldn't see a tiny embryo among the tissue that would soon pass from my body, comforted me. I hadn't done anything wrong. This miscarriage, this loss, had been weeks in the making. From the moment conception occurred, the complex mixture of genes, DNA, chromosomes, and all the elements of our primordial soup that need to be *just right* to create a tiny bean of a baby, hadn't been right after all.

I *had* been pregnant. My body had produced hCG in its beautifully natural response to the tiny attempt at life nestled in my womb. I had become a mother, because although the amazingly attuned evolutionary system in my body recognized quickly the unsustainability of the pregnancy, that message was delayed in getting to my brain. The powerful hormonal elixir of estrogen and oxytocin worked its magic, unaware that while it began the process of creating a mother, another bodily system was preparing for the end.

I was already changing, physically and emotionally. And even though this brief spark of life, this tiny grain of sand, would soon pass through my body, my body and spirit would be forever changed. The cells and chemicals of my body had been transformed. Our bodies are constantly dying and being reborn through cellular renewal and breathing and living. Though new life hadn't been created this time, something had been born.

I realized that although I wouldn't be cradling a baby in seven months, I had become a mother.

*****

Grief and suffering are universal. But how we grieve and how suffering manifests itself is as unique as each of the 7 billion people on our planet. In my grief, I found comfort in science, in learning about exactly what had happened in my body, why it happened, and how common my experience was. If I had faith in anything, it was statistics. The statistics told me I was not alone and reassured me that not only was another pregnancy likely, but it would be healthy and normal.

I learned that a blighted ovum (or anembryonic gestation) is the most common form of early pregnancy loss. By some estimates, it is the reason for half of all first-trimester miscarriages. If you are experiencing an early loss, it may be due to an anembryonic pregnancy.

And it's a terrible sounding name, isn't it? While the notion that there hadn't been a baby comforted me, it can be terribly painful to be told you've had a "non-baby" pregnancy. The sister term "early pregnancy failure" is no better. The clinical terms of the medical community as they describe the physical manifestations of our hopes and dreams can be devastating. I strongly believe our words matter, and the medical terms where women's bodies are concerned are often wounding.

We all grieve differently. I think part of that grief is owning and reclaiming how *we* conceptualize that loss, free from medical jargon and culturally loaded terms like "failure." If you want to embrace your loss as your angel baby, then claim, remember, and honor your angel baby. An embryo may not have developed, but conception occurred. However brief, the spark of life was alive inside you.

But if you don't want to call it your angel baby, if you don't even think of your loss as the loss of a baby, that's okay, too. *And you are not alone.* Though many resources and websites and grieving mothers will speak of angel babies, you can name and own your grief in the way that resonates with your worldview and comforts you.

I didn't do anything, nor do I do anything today, to memorialize the miscarriage (though I did keep the positive pregnancy tests for a long time, as if I needed confirmation, a reminder, that I really had been pregnant, and that even though that terrible ultrasound only showed a collapsing uterine lining, *something* about the pregnancy had been real, even if it was only a few pink lines that yellowed with age).

Because the pain and grief were real.

But if I didn't think I was losing a baby, what was I grieving?

I didn't even know.

*****

I can see it a lot more clearly now, with the events of that summer in the rearview mirror, eight years into my continuing journey of motherhood, and along a new spiritual path that has introduced me to yoga, meditation, and Buddhism.

I don't think we can have plans for grief the way we map out escapes from our homes in the case of fire, though the panic and desire to flee the inferno and conflagration of sorrow may feel quite similar.

But I do have words of advice I would love to have been able to share with the me that was sobbing, alone at home, alone with her confused grief, and alone, with her husband an ocean away. I don't know if she would have understood it then. But I think it may have helped her.

Buddhism teaches that life is suffering, and pain and loss and grief are universal. And we suffer because we crave, we desire, and we attach ourselves to people and dreams. When we lose those things, which we inevitably will, for nothing is permanent, we suffer.

A Buddhist approach to grief would ask, "What have you actually lost?" And this is a tough question for early pregnancy loss or child loss, for at least with the loss of a loved one at the end of a long life, we have memories, stories, and mementos to hold onto. With a pregnancy or child, it is the loss of a dream. A vision of that dear baby, a picture of ourselves in our new life as a mother.

I would tell the grieving me, "*Your loss counts.* The moment you became pregnant, you thought of yourself as a mother. You don't have to grieve a baby, but you can grieve the loss of a dream."

Buddhism teaches us that grief is universal; we cannot avoid or ignore it, nor should we try to. When we are grieving, we must acknowledge it and feel it. Even if people tell us to "move on," for a time we must simply sit with our anguish. And each day our grief itself changes; some days will be better, while other days the pain will come back with unbearable force.

Sometimes all we can do is sit with our suffering, embrace it, breathe through it, and hold ourselves with compassion. And know that, like all other things, *this too shall pass*. But it will pass in its own time, not according to anyone else's schedule.

Buddhism also teaches us to practice mindfulness—nonjudgmental awareness of the present moment. We may be grieving, but is there joy and beauty too? This doesn't mean we ignore pain, nor does it mean we view the world through rose-colored glasses. But beauty and transformation can coexist with suffering.

I know in my darkest moments after my miscarriage, I was not at all interested in "finding a silver lining."

But from my vantage point now, I know those months of bereavement had meaning. For many years prior to becoming pregnant, I never thought I would become a mother. I told myself I did not want children. After my miscarriage, even though I don't believe in "signs," I wondered, was this a sign that I really wasn't meant to be a mom?

But the intensity of my grief, after living for just a few weeks with that dream of motherhood, reassured me that, yes, I do want to be a mom. I found the clarity in my maternal longing that had not been there before. It was real. I desired—and, yes, even craved—motherhood.

*****

Oh, there's so much I want to tell years-ago-grieving me. I want to hop into an Einsteinian wormhole and arrive in that painful summer. I want to show her a different version of *It's a Wonderful Life*:

a time-lapse video of how she will continue to change and evolve in her journey to become a mother.

I imagine the stars, the *universe,* speaking to her as Clarence spoke to George Bailey. And through her grief, she watches the following images in vibrant color:

Her motherhood journey begins with a joyous restaurant celebration in Tuscany, family members showering her in love and hugs and very early belly rubs. Then cut to the scene where she enters the dark forest, an all-too-early initiation into the rite of childbirth and pain and the agony of loss.

Then we see grief ebb and flow; we see life proceed. Summer becomes fall, and she's back at work, living her life. Then we see her, huddled inside during a cold January, calling her mother with the news of a new pregnancy, and the dream is reborn. We see her next ultrasound, which reveals a melodious heartbeat. We see morning sickness and maternity clothes and baby showers...and then it's the beginning of another fall. Her sister is marrying the young man with them in the Italian restaurant, another celebration of life and love. We see the big-bellied, radiant maid of honor next to the bride, her bouquet held just above her daughter ensconced in the protection of her womb. And then it's the joyously tearful moment, with the bundled new arrival placed in her awaiting mother's arms. It's Abigail. For this is the dream...

There was no angel baby, but there had been a dream of motherhood. A dream of motherhood lost, and now reborn. And a few years later, the same dream, the universal primordial dream in which our maternal desire and ambivalence and joy and suffering are all one, is reborn again in her beautiful son.

I hope she understands. She was always a mother. She is always changing, being reborn. She still continues the forever letting go that is the universal path of motherhood, whether the babies are angels, dreams, animated breath, or a sacred trinity of all three. She was a mother from the moment the universal light settled briefly in her.

It *is* a wonderful life. She isn't just dreaming.

Sincerely,
Sarah

"Buddhism teaches us that grief is universal; we cannot avoid or ignore it, nor should we try to."

—Sarah Rudell Beach

"I had lost my daughter and all of the hopes and dreams I had for her, and now I felt like I was losing God and my faith—and if I lost that, I was afraid I would lose myself."

—Kristi Bothur

A Parent's Love

I can't believe this happened
Throughout the pregnancy you seemed fine,
All outwardly signs perfect
Oh precious child of mine.

All ten fingers and ten toes
Lined up in sweet little rows,
Your nose, your lips, your face
Adorable, and forming at perfect pace.

But for some unknown reason,
A part of you did not grow.
And because of this anomaly, this world you will
never know.

Had we let nature take its course,
Your mom and dad would have led a life of
remorse,
Because had we let you been born this way,
You would have suffered severely every day.

We put you first and ourselves last,
In hopes we could end your pain fast.
For the greatest love a parent can display
Is to take their child's agony away.

— Dana W.

She Ran Away from the Lord

By Jennie Goutet

"Okay, God," my husband said, as he scanned the streets crammed with the New Year's Eve festivities, "I pray you find us a great parking spot right by Fred's apartment."

I looked out my window at the lights from the shops and apartment buildings spilling out onto the sidewalk. "Yeah right," I muttered under my breath, "like *He* answers prayers."

I was probably not in the best shape to be attending a New Year's Eve party, even a small gathering with just close friends. It had not been a week since I stood in the shower at three in the morning and pulled out the gray, lifeless body of my baby. Not even a week to get used to my new emptiness.

God and I had been through things in the past. I grieved my brother's suicide numbly, my heart torn in shreds, as I went through the motions of living for two years. But I didn't know God yet when I went through that, and I thought I was walking through the valley of the shadow of death alone. I grieved the deaths of the orphans in Africa where we were living, and the businessmen and women in the Twin Towers from the city we left behind I thought I had perspective on grief.

But the miscarriage? My mourning was laced with feelings of betrayal because I had trusted that God would see me through. There was a scripture in Exodus I had found a few weeks before the loss, which helped me to trust God despite the fear of getting pregnant in my forties. It helped me to trust Him when the baby's tests came back with the possibility of Down's syndrome.

When I read, "I will take away sickness from among you, and none will miscarry or be barren in your land. I will give you a full life span" (1), I thought He was talking to me.

"Thank you, God," I whispered as I read this. "Thank you for the promise you've made me." And with His assurance, I laid all my fears to rest. I believed His promise so wholly, when the midwife told me there was no heartbeat, I didn't believe it. I kept expecting to receive a call later that afternoon to tell me the machine was faulty and that I should come back to the hospital for a second opinion.

My friends welcomed me at the New Year's Eve party with sympathy I did not want. I didn't want to see people's faces fall, their mouths forming little "Oohs" of compassion when I entered the room. I wanted to punch someone instead. But when Isabelle sat on the arm of the couch and rubbed my back without saying a word, tears fell silently down my face. My husband saw us from across the room, and thought, *Good. She's getting what she needs.*

I know that God is approachable. He allowed Abraham to negotiate with Him about whether or not to spare Sodom and Gomorrah; He allowed Abraham to approach Him *six times* in his pleading for this wicked city (2). He listened when Hezekiah turned his face to the wall and begged God to spare him when told he was going to die (3). He strengthened Elijah when the enemies had pursued him until he had no more courage left. And then the Lord showed Himself to Elijah — not in the earthquake or the fire or in the great wind. No, God came in the gentle whisper (4).

Sometimes in loss, it can feel more like we're dealing with the God who answered Job out of a storm, "Who is this that darkens my counsel with words without knowledge? Brace yourself like a man; I will question you, and you shall answer me" (5).

In the storm of our loss, we can feel like we're at the whim of a merciless God who demands our complete obedience but offers absolutely no promises to help us understand *why* this is happening. "I wouldn't even treat my own kid this way," we think.

Then the negotiations begin. Like the armies Jesus talked about — the one of 10,000 going up against an army twice its size (6) — we face the fact that we're never going to win. His army is bigger than ours. "God is God," we say, "so I just need to shut my mouth and revere Him." I need to give Him glory, and I will do just that. Never mind that my teeth are clenched so tightly that they're about to break. Never mind that there are no tears left, no more curling up at His feet, no more lifting my face to His in earnest love and gratitude. We stop talking about how we feel, and we just…accept what He's done. In fact, we stop talking to Him completely.

Jonah was a small prophet in the Bible, with only four chapters to his name, and yet he is so important, every single child has heard about someone being swallowed by a large fish (even if they're thinking of Pinocchio and his father). Jonah is so important, Jesus mentioned him, saying he was a sign of what was to come (7). And yet this was not a guy who was supposedly "doing well spiritually." He was a real person with human flaws.

When God asked Jonah to go preach to the city of Nineveh so that they would turn away from their sins and be saved, Jonah headed to Tarshish instead. This city was actually in the opposite direction of where he was supposed to go — the remotest destination he had access to. I suppose Jonah's reaction was not that surprising, considering the Assyrians, whose capital was found in Nineveh, were a brutal people and had oppressed Israel for years. Preaching to them a plan of God's mercy was not exactly something Jonah could throw his heart behind.

When we suffer loss, and especially when we suffer loss as a mother, the outpouring of our grief can result in a refusal to continue to deal with God. After all, He's the one that ordained the loss. He's the one who allowed it to pass. Either that, or He has absolutely no power at all. (But that's a different sort of questioning, and it has its place in a different discussion.)

In Jonah's story, he is sleeping in the boat headed to Tarshish when a violent storm comes — a storm so fierce that the ship threatens to break into pieces. Not even a churning boat and the terrified cries of the sailors could rouse Jonah from his slumber. It took the captain of the ship — a nonbeliever — to come and beseech him to call upon his God so that perhaps they would be saved.

I kind of get Jonah sleeping through it all. The year we lived in Africa was pretty intense, and the night someone set a bomb off in the compound next door, I slept right through the commotion. I didn't hear a thing. When we feel overwhelmed, sleep comes as a relief — an escape. In grief, it's sometimes the only relief we get.

When the sailors confronted Jonah, his response was rather extreme. Rather than praying to a God he knew could save him, he stoically commanded the sailors, "Pick me up and throw me into the sea, and it will become calm." He preferred suicide to prayer, which, when you think about it, come on, Jonah! Is it really so bad you'd rather die than pray?

But he remained firm, and as soon as the sailors tossed him overboard, the raging sea grew calm. But God did not allow Jonah to die; He had different plans for him. He provided a big fish to swallow him, and Jonah stayed inside the fish three days and three nights.

So basically, Jonah stewed in the belly of a big stinking fish for three days and three nights because he hadn't wanted to pray. His refusal to deal directly with God was not helping his life to get any easier.

My recovery from the miscarriage was laughably convoluted and long. After the hemorrhage that occurred at home and continued in the car and in the emergency room, the doctors decided that my body had taken care of everything on its own. But the follow-up ultrasounds, prescribed by my own doctor in the weeks to come, revealed that there were still open blood vessels — most likely a piece of the umbilical cord that was still attached.

Over the weeks that followed, we tried everything to resolve the issue without surgery, including three rounds of medicine to cause contractions. Each time, the ultrasound would reveal that there was still debris in the womb, despite the copious bleeding that always followed the treatment. The last trial turned into an all-out hemorrhage that sent me back to the emergency room, where they assured me, once again, my body had taken care of everything by itself and I didn't need surgery.

My bitter, venomous grief that followed the miscarriage had calmed into a sort of cold indifference as the weeks rolled out. Every time there was a new development that left me physically uncomfortable and unable to heal emotionally, I would give a humorless laugh and turn my face away from God. *As if the miscarriage weren't enough,* I thought to myself, *you're doing this, too.* I knew I needed to obey God. I knew He was my Lord and my Savior, but I no longer considered Him my friend.

Jonah was forced to take stock of his new, uncomfortable surroundings, and he had an outward change of heart. He decided to pray, and that's when he *finally* spoke to God directly, promising, "What I have vowed, I will make good" (8).

The fish vomited Jonah out on dry land, where he proceeded to head back to Nineveh. This large city normally required three days to cross it, and Jonah was supposed to warn the entire city. But he only ventured partway into the city for one day, and gave them all a resounding hellfire and damnation speech that little resembled God's plan for grace. And despite his halfhearted prophecy, the result was unexpected. Everyone in the city repented of his sins, from the greatest to the least.

In my own life, post-loss, I was going through the spiritual motions, as if everything had not been turned upside down. I was still going to church, and we were still hosting the weekly Bible discussion group at our house. I was still teaching the Bible to people, because "this is what God expects me to do." But I never really got the feeling he cared how I felt, and I was just going through the motions.

When Jonah saw that God had relented from bringing calamity on a people he despised, he was greatly displeased. He went out and sat at a place east of the city, where he built a shelter to give him shade. Then he waited to see what would happen to the city.

I can just see God watching him act like a recalcitrant child, watching him and loving him. God provided a vine to grow up over Jonah's head to give him shade and ease his discomfort as he sat there. And Jonah was very happy about the vine.

When it was clear that my body could not remove the debris left behind by the baby on its own and a D & C was finally scheduled, I was overwhelmed with relief. "Now I'm going to have closure on this whole awful business," I told my friends. "I'll finally be able to move forward." I canceled all of the children's activities in preparation, and I asked my in-laws to watch them overnight. And then I canceled my English classes so I would have a completely free day to go to the hospital and take care of my needs. The upcoming procedure was like shade — a respite from the hot sun of grief, a promise that things were finally going my way.

But in Jonah's story, the shady vine that brought relief did not last. God provided a worm the next day that chewed the vine so that it withered. And then He sent a scorching wind that blazed on Jonah's head until he felt faint. Gah! Goaded beyond what he could bear by this seemingly inconsequential event, Jonah said, "It would be better for me to die than to live."

Really, Jonah? You want to die over a *vine?* After you've gone through a shipwreck and sat in the belly of a whale, you're upset about a little *shade?* His reaction was completely disproportionate to the event that caused it.

In my own story, the night before I was supposed to go in, the hospital left a message saying they had no time to take me the next morning, and I would need to come back in a week's time. And *that* was the last straw. Goaded by the horrible loss, the betrayal I felt from God, the months of heavy bleeding, and now this last inconvenience, I just lost it. I was furious.

God said to Jonah, "Do you have a right to be angry about the vine?" (9).

And Jonah replied, "I do. I am angry enough to die."

Ah. So now we've gotten to the crux of the matter. He finally said it. He said, I am *angry.* I am so angry, I could die.

He lost all perspective over a piece of shade because he was angry. He ran away from God because he hadn't articulated the fact that he was angry. God led him inexorably to the point where he finally expressed what was on his heart. And no matter how ridiculous his reactions were for a supposed "man of God," at no point did God rebuke him for the way he was feeling. God's mercy was complete.

Sometimes I think our hardships, post-loss, come as God pushes and pushes until our hearts scream out in grief at the *injustice* of it all, "I am angry enough to die!"

But when we express it, we are in a place where He can go in and heal the hurt. Jonah healed after he expressed it. He had to; otherwise, how could he have told a story that glorified God's great mercy, while making himself look so much like a fool that the result is comical? He could not have glorified God if he were still seething in unexpressed anger.

There came a time when I grew tired of being angry and I wanted my relationship with God back. I confided to a friend that I had no idea how to stop being so mad at God. I had no idea how to move forward in my relationship with Him anymore. I didn't even know how to start talking to Him, or how to trust Him again.

And she reminded me of this:

For men are not cast off by the Lord forever.

Though he brings grief, he will show compassion, so great is his unfailing love.

For he does not willingly bring affliction or grief to the children of men.

Lamentations 3:31-33 (NIV)

The Lord is God. I can't dispute that. My own efforts at being lord of my own life have been laughable at best and most often tragic. But we are not following a God who makes decisions about our lives ruthlessly, coldheartedly, with snide comments to "just suck it up." We are following a tenderhearted God, who "gently leads those who have young" (10), whose "eyes will weep bitterly, overflowing with tears, because the Lord's flock will be taken captive" (11), a God who does not *willingly* bring affliction or grief.

God can handle it when we rage. He will even push us to rage, to get us to express it so that it brings us relief and healing. But unless we remember who God really is, we won't heal spiritually. And our emotional healing will take that much longer.

The day I finally surrendered was just another ordinary day. It was still cold out, and I was sitting on our couch, covered with a red tartan wool blanket, the epitome of comfort for me. The anger had been a festering boil that prevented me from healing, but that day I sat, studying the scripture in Lamentations until it pierced my heart.

"God," I said, struggling, "I don't want to live without you. I have nothing without you. I *am* nothing without you. Through my whole life, and even through my troubles, you have showered me with blessing upon blessing. I don't understand why I had to lose my baby, but I know *you*. And I know with certainty that you do not willingly bring grief or affliction to my life. And *this* is a promise I can hold on to. This is a promise meant for me."

As I prayed, I began to cry for the first time since I'd lost my baby. I wept, and the poison bled from the wound in my soul, gouged out by grief and anger. I healed, and I was able to lift my eyes to His face once more. I trusted again, and set my hopes fully on the love of my God and my Friend.

Blessings,
Jennie

All Scripture quoted is from the NIV:
Exodus 23:25b-26
Genesis 18:20-33
2 Kings 20:1-11
1 Kings 19:9-12
Job 38:1-3
Luke 14:31-32
Luke 11-29-32
Jonah 2:9b
Jonah 4:9
Isaiah 40:11
Jeremiah 13:17

"Anger is an important phase of grief, even though it is one of the most misunderstood. It will hold you up and carry you through some of the worst times. Embrace it, feel it, let it help you, and then find a way to work past it so that you can truly heal."

—Kelly DeBie

Faith and Loss: Finding Your Way Back

By Kristi Bothur

I am a Christian, raised in a Christian family. I have followed Jesus closely since childhood. I met my husband in seminary. I can't remember a time when I didn't believe in God. Since my teenage years, I have been committed to sharing the Gospel with others, being absolutely convinced of the truth of God's Word. I'm the wife of a pastor, a former missionary, and Jesus is my life, in every sense.

Then my daughter died, and it almost all fell apart.

I lost Naomi when I was 18 weeks pregnant, and at first, shock kept me in a safe, protective bubble. In my bubble, I could still have faith and tell people that of course I was sad, but I knew God had a plan and I was okay with whatever His plan was. In my bubble I could cry but still trust, and people around us remarked at my strong faith. I would nod numbly, because that was how someone with faith should act, right?

The bubble lasted about a week before it burst. Suddenly I felt like I was drowning, and the faith that I had embraced since I was a child was no longer tethering me to the shore. I was angry, scared, sad, confused, and completely devastated. All I wanted was my baby. I felt like God had turned His back on me. Suddenly nothing I had believed about Him made sense, and that terrified me. I had lost my daughter and all of the hopes and dreams I had for her, and now I felt like I was losing God and my faith—and if I lost that, I was afraid I would lose myself. But not only that, I needed to know what the truth was, one way or the other. Was my childhood faith based on something real, or did I need to learn a new way to live?

Thus began a voyage of not only grieving for my daughter, but struggling for my faith. Today, more than four years later, my faith is stronger but also different. Hopefully it is more mature, more grounded, more tested, and more secure. In some ways it is more jaded and less patient with those who would throw Scripture at the wounded instead of applying it carefully, with love.

If you are struggling with your faith in the days and months and even years after losing a child, please know how completely normal that is. No guilt, okay? Not everyone questions God after a loss, but there's no special medal if you don't. In fact, the Bible is full of people who got mad at God and accused Him of being unfair and unloving. If that is true for you, too—well, you aren't the first and you won't be the last, and He can handle it.

Just as there is no one way to grieve, there is also no one path from questioning and doubt back to faith again. But there are some steps you can take on the journey that were helpful to me that I would like to share with you.

First, do what you can to clarify the questions and issues you are having. I started off confused about how, if He loved me, God could allow my daughter to die, when He could have easily saved her life. Was He not powerful, or not loving? Then I realized that I was not really questioning God's power. I knew He could have saved Naomi; that was part of the problem. Why didn't He? Didn't His love require Him to keep His children from experiencing such great pain? If not, what kind of love does He have? Realizing what I was struggling with made it easier to look for relevant answers.

Are you struggling with trusting God? With anger at Him, or at those who follow Him? Are you struggling with fear, or are you doubting His existence altogether? If you can clarify *what* you are struggling with and *why* (e.g., I'm having a hard time trusting God because He didn't save my baby's life, and I don't know if He will protect me in the future), it will be easier to start looking for answers.

Second, do those things that people of faith do. Hang out with God's people. Keep praying. Read the Scriptures. Even if you feel like a hypocrite, keep doing it. Not because it matches where your heart is, but because that is where you will find the truth — about God and eternity and yourself.

Very soon after losing Naomi, I found an online ministry called Hannah's Prayer, which provides community forums to married Christian women struggling with fertility issues, whether through infertility or pregnancy and infant loss. There I encountered women who modeled for me how it was possible to lose a child and still have a relationship with God. Others around me in "real life" did the same, including a Christian grief counselor who had also experienced pregnancy loss and my best friend, who had lost a baby not long before Naomi died. I read books about loss, written by women of faith who could point me in the direction I needed to go. All of these gave me hope that I could survive with my faith intact.

I devoured passages in the Bible that talked about unborn babies, loss, grief, God's love, faith, trust. I camped out in the Psalms for a long time, in Hebrews 11, and from time to time in Job. I was desperate to know what God thought of my baby girl, and I needed to know if I could ever trust Him again. I knew that the Bible held the answers.

At the same time, guard your heart. If the people in your church or fellowship group or Bible study are saying or doing things that are constantly causing hurt and reopening the wound in your heart, you don't have to keep exposing yourself to that. If the women's prayer group you are in has a dozen pregnant women in it constantly complaining about morning sickness, you don't have to keep going. I'm not saying that you should leave your church if someone hurts your feelings, but if you are in a situation where your heart is getting more and more bitter because of the reactions of people around you, it's okay to remove yourself from that situation and seek out a healthier one. It's also okay to take a break from church for a while, or not to go on days that just hurt your heart, like Mother's Day.

If you decide to take a break from your church, or from all churches, for a while, however, do take a couple of extra steps. First, honestly examine yourself to understand why you want a break; if God is trying to get your attention about something, you don't want to run from that. Second, do seek out spiritual nourishment somewhere else while you give your emotions a rest. And third, put an end date on your break. Decide when you will return, or you may find that it is easier to stay away. If you decide not to return to your church, find another one. God's plan for us is to be in community with others who call on His name. Don't give up on that. He has a place for you.

Finally, don't settle. Don't settle for holding God at arm's length. Don't settle for surface answers to deep questions or just going through the motions. Push forward. Seek God vigorously, as if your life depended on it—because it does. In Jeremiah 29, God promised the Israelites in exile that if they would seek Him with all their heart, they would find Him. That promise is true for us, too, who find ourselves "exiled" to the land of Loss. God is not hiding from us. He longs to be our comfort and our Savior, to fill our lives with purpose and hope, even in the midst of our greatest heartache.

Keep asking, keep seeking, keep knocking (Matthew 7:7), and you will find your way back. And when you do, you will find, as I did, that the One waiting for you is worthy of your trust and worship, not because

He promises a life free of trouble and sorrow, but because He is who He is—full of love and fully sovereign and ready to reveal to you how He can redeem this, your deepest heartache, for your good and His glory.

God Bless,
Kristi

"I always knew God would protect me from 'the fire.' I never knew that fire would be the fire of my own anger."

—Rachel Raper

A Crisis and Faith

By Heather O'Brien Webb

My husband and I each had a crisis of faith, in the week after Clara was born still at 42 weeks and 3 days gestation.

My husband David was raised a Baptist; to believe in God, Jesus, heaven and hell. There are a thousand ways to go to hell and one very narrow path to heaven's gates. He was taught to believe that when a loved one dies, it was just "their time" and that "they were called home" and other platitudes intended to give comfort. He went through the loss of his uncle dying when we were in high school, and three years ago, he lost his aunt. He dealt with these deaths by falling back on his lifelong Baptist training; they are there waiting for him to join them, when it's his time, and they will all be reunited.

I was raised to question the beliefs that the majority of the Southern population hold dear. I was raised agnostic, raised to believe that there might be *something* out there, but we don't know what it is. Over time, I have become less agnostic and more atheist. I don't believe in God or Jesus or heaven or hell. I believe that when a loved one dies, they are dead, and the only way they live on is in our hearts and memories, not in some arbitrary "beyond."

I lost my best friend Patsy in 2007, and at the funeral, the preacher said something about walking on streets of gold, and that "if she could choose to come back to Earth, she would turn down the offer, because she is in a better place now." Immediately I thought that he didn't know *what* he was talking about. There is no way that my friend would *choose* to be *anywhere* else except with her seven children. These are the things people tell themselves to feel better in the face of loss, but it brings me no comfort.

After Clara died, though, David was no longer so sure of his beliefs, and neither was I.

I desperately wanted to believe in the things that he was taught to believe. I wanted to believe that my baby was in heaven with her great-grandma, who would rock her and care for her until her daddy and I are, one day, able to join them. I wanted to believe that Clara's great-grandpa, great-uncle, and great-aunt are with our sweet girl. I wanted to, because it's a beautiful thought, but I really don't believe that, deep down. I have always felt like it must be such a comfort to "give it up to God" and feel that "God will always provide." I have felt jealousy, at times, of those who have such blind faith, because I just don't believe that.

David, on the other hand, realized that his long-held beliefs weren't bringing the same comfort he'd come to expect. He still believes in God, but the idea of our daughter being an "angel baby" who is watching over us from a cloud in the sky? Not so much. He's discontented with the notion that "she was too perfect for Earth, so Jesus took her to heaven," and he's angry at the idea that this happened "for a reason." It wasn't "supposed to be this way," or any of the other things that well-meaning people say to try and make us feel better. I think his family was afraid that living with an atheist would steer him from the spiritual path that they believe is right. In the end, something completely out of my hands shook his faith.

It is a natural human need to explain things, and religion is one result of that need. Believers perceive the afterlife as being "as real as flesh." Wars are fought in the name of God, and laws are written to conform with God's will. But of all the faithful who carve out the world as they believe God wants it to be, most forget that the most important function of faith is, well, faith in the endurance of our immortal souls. Religion is a deeply personal thing, and there is no *one* right way to believe.

David and I have talked a lot since our baby died. We want to understand why this happened to us, but have come to feel that there is no why. Some things just happen, with no rhyme, no reason; no promise or punishment. Neither of us is completely confident in what we believe now, and that's just as okay as feeling absolutely sure of one belief system or another. We know that we have each other to bounce ideas and feelings off of, without judgment.

Nothing makes the loss of Clara *better,* but we're reaching a point where we are able to celebrate the little time we had with her, rather than mourn the time we weren't able to have with her.

Through our crisis, tears and sadness a faith in each other has emerged, stronger than it has ever been before.

Sincerely,

Heather

"After Clara died, though, David was no longer so sure of his beliefs, and neither was I. I desperately wanted to believe in the things that he was taught to believe. I wanted to believe that my baby was in heaven with her great-grandma Edith, who would rock her and make sure she was well cared for until her daddy and I are, one day, able to join them."

—Heather Webb

I Thought

I thought I would find solace
In this holy place,
Instead I found just emptiness,
And a loneliness unbearable to face.

I thought connecting with my religion
Would help me find my way,
But each sacred word that was spoken
Seemed to cause me to further drift away.

The prayers discussed "from birth to death"
But with you it wasn't that way,
You never experienced a single breath
Thus there is no "official" place for your memory
to lay.

I thought my house of worship
Would ease my pain somehow,
Instead it has left me feeling detached
And full of confusion now.

— Dana Weinstein

"Despite my anger and grief, I DO believe in the power of prayer. I remember the calmness and almost a sense of quiet peace that came over me as I lay in that hospital bed, day after day, pregnant, waiting and hoping for a miracle that my babies would live. I remember when I came to peace with the fact that Kathryn would die."

—Alexa Bigwarfe

My Ministry: Embracing Evan

By Rachel Raper

I am a child of God. I am a wife. I am a mother of two. I am brokenhearted. I have hope. I have faith.

I don't believe in coincidences, but I do believe in God. My story has twists and turns; my grief has ups and downs, but it always includes my faith in Christ. I won't tell you what to believe, but instead what I believe. I believe that God knew that I would incur the loss of a child. I believe that He set up blessings and a support system that has allowed me to endure the loss of Evan and to grow a new ministry, Embracing Evan. Here is my story.

We learned on December 18, 2011, that we were going to expand our family and give our daughter Whitney a sibling. We learned April 2, 2012, that our second child was a boy who we had decided to name Evan. Little did we know that that ultrasound would be our only time seeing life in our son Evan. I felt him squirm, kick, and wiggle as I carried this precious gift for 36 weeks. I wish that I could tell you why, but all of that movement ceased, and so did the life of my child.

After learning Evan would be stillborn, over the coming hours on July 24, 2012, I believe that God put in place influential people who positively influenced the first steps of our grief journey. I believe the timing of each encounter was not coincidence, but God's perfect timing.

While in labor with Evan, my pastor and his wife were present in my hospital room. I was in shock and denial, and I was hesitant. I was hesitant to question God and hesitant to be angry with Him. In those hours, my pastor's words gave me permission to feel angry, which allowed me to step briefly out of my sense of denial that served as my temporary shield to pain.

After giving birth to Evan, my husband Derek and I were visited by a dear friend. Our feelings of love and pride for our boy were able to be shared, and joy that was not overshadowed by our sorrow spilled forth from our lips as the three of us admired Evan in the hospital room.

After twelve hours with Evan in our arms and by our side, it was time to leave his body behind at the hospital and move on to some altered life we were unsure of. At this time, God prepared a visit from our Sunday school teacher. In his words, we found the strength to face the unthinkable. We gave one last kiss and one last look, and said good-bye. In that moment, God was present, too.

The next day, while making decisions at the funeral home, we had one more visitor that God had put into place for us. It was the pastor who married Derek and me. He was a part-time employee, who was still at the funeral home after his shift had ended. None of us knew we would be meeting under those circumstances that day. Our past pastor was able to minister to us at another pivotal point in our grief journey because he had experienced the loss of a child not once, but twice. Again, I don't believe in coincidences, but I do believe in God.

One must know that having faith doesn't replace grief, and having joy in life certainly doesn't erase grief. After I experienced death, that was a part of me, housed within my womb, I realized how precious and fragile life was. Through blurred eyes and a foggy mind, I became more thankful of the life of my daughter, and I found hope to live to be a good mommy for Whitney, the living child, whose time was still with me on Earth.

Although I experienced days in the depths of despair the following months, I had a glimmer of hope. Currently, I am choosing to walk a life of faith. I am choosing a healthy path of reconstruction and repair for myself and family as I am learning acceptance. I am even choosing to face my fears and try for my third pregnancy. Through my experience, I have been humbled. I have learned that although I am strong, I am not strong enough. I need the power of Christ.

My goal is to encourage parents who have been affected by the loss of a child, so that they may find faith, keep faith, or grow their faith—for faith brings joy. In joy, I mean rejoicing in the creation of the child we lost to death, to value and appreciate the time we have with our children here on Earth, and to rejoice and be glad that God is faithful, for we will see our children again in heaven. Lamentations 3:31-33 says, "For the Lord does not abandon anyone forever. Though he brings grief, he also shows compassion according to the greatness of his unfailing love. For he does not enjoy hurting people or causing them sorrow."

Our lives have suffered great grief; we have felt abandoned, and our hearts have been filled with overwhelming sorrow. However, just as God sent visitors to Derek and me in the first hours of our grief, God had already prepared a visitor, of sorts, for all who believe. This visitor is the Holy Spirit. On July 24, 2012, in my womb, I carried death; in my heart, I carried the promise of comfort from God through the Holy Spirit. Second Corinthians 1:3-4 says, "Praise be to the God and Father of our Lord Jesus Christ, the Father of compassion and the God of all comfort, who comforts us in all our troubles, so that we can comfort those in any trouble with the comfort we ourselves receive from God."

Leaving the hospital only twelve hours after Evan's stillbirth left an unexplainable sense of shock, emptiness, and bewilderment. My arms and womb were empty, and my heart was broken. Matthew 5:4 says, "God blesses those who mourn, for they will be comforted." I was comforted by the Holy Spirit; I was comforted by the kind words and actions of others who were lead through prayer to be my comfort.

I believe that we should comfort those in need. It is the needs of others who are searching for hope and comfort in the midst of tragedy that birthed my ministry, Embracing Evan. The Embracing Evan ministry has teamed with Mommy to Mommy Outreach, which is supported by Naomi's Circle to provide huggable teddy bears to mothers who have just experienced the loss of a child through miscarriage, stillborn, or infant death while hospitalized at Lexington Medical Center, Richland Memorial Hospital, and Palmetto Health Baptist Hospital in Columbia, South Carolina.

Mommy to Mommy Outreach has donated fifty Brie Bags, each complete with one blue or pink Embracing Evan bear, since April 2013. We are saddened that other women experience loss that creates a continued need, but we are excited that these valuable resources will be in the hands and arms of others to comfort their hearts. These bears are for each mom to hold, hug, and rock in their initial moments of pain. My prayer is that they receive the message of hope, because as a mommy who has experienced great loss, I have learned that you cannot bear it alone.

Love,
Rachel

"I guess my happiness was ultimately found online, helping others... Actually, the first time I felt like I was happy in a making-progress way was about three months out when I came up to bed after spending hours online and my husband asked what I'd been doing, and I said I was talking to another mom who just had a loss and I felt like I'd helped her. I felt like I'd been able to pull her up a bit, in the same way other women had helped pull me up early on when I just couldn't see any light...."

—Tova Gold

Chapter 6: Changed Perspectives and Relationships

A loss of this nature impacts relationships, sometimes in a very major way. You may be completely changed as an individual, which often results in a shift in the people who are your inner circle. There is a good chance that you will become closely connected to other grieving mothers and you will develop new relationships with different people.

Relationships with your spouse/partner can also change drastically. This is the topic for Chapter Seven, so we will not cover that important element here.

As a group we discussed the hurtful things that were said (or not said) by some of our closest friends and family members. One mother talked about the fact that her best friend sent her a text saying, "Sooo sorry," and she did not contact her again for two weeks! Another contributor told us how she has not talked to her best friend since losing her baby almost six years ago. As she stated it, "I guess she did not know what to say, so she just didn't say anything at all."

We share our tips on how loss and grief changes your perspectives and relationships, some for the worse and some for the better.

"One piece of advice I would give myself would be to be open to the new friendships that will spring up out of the loss. Of course I was happy with my old friends before Jack died. I was happy with my life, too. But I learned that some people will be better equipped than others at stepping into this new reality with us. If I had decided I didn't have enough room in my heart for any new friends, I would have missed out on some rich, meaningful relationships."

—Anna Whiston-Donaldson

The Two Tracks

By Anna Donaldson

Yesterday I dropped my eleven-year-old daughter Margaret off to board a bus for a middle-school church retreat several hours away. She was anxious about being so far from home and so was I, but after some deep breathing and encouragement, she bravely climbed on the bus with her friends.

As the parents formed a circle and prayed in the parking lot for safe travels and for God to bless the retreat, tears streamed down my face. I tried to hide them behind my sunglasses so Margaret would be neither freaked out nor embarrassed as she looked out the bus window. Of course she saw me. My friend Jenn gave me a hug and said, "She's going to be fine."

I buried my head in her shoulder and managed to choke out, "I'm not crying about Margaret."

She answered, "I know."

So many moments in life that should be easy and joyful are brutal and difficult now. The parking lot is just one small example of the little battles and struggles that weave their way through every single day of loss for a bereaved parent. For me, it is the pain I feel with anything involving adolescent boys. I see them everywhere in their short haircuts and big sneakers and want to say, "Why? Why us? Why our son?" For others, it could the sight of a pregnant belly or a baby. Or Wednesdays. Or hospitals. Or the 8th of the month. Or rainy days. Or summertime. Or the grocery store. Don't even get me started on the grocery store. It is as if our brains are always operating on two separate tracks, and the integration of these tracks could take a lifetime.

One track is the here and now of living and loving and going to school or to work, but there is always the parallel track of loss and what could have been yet will not be. My son Jack should have been on that bus with his beloved sister. But he wasn't. Because one warm day I let my kids play outside in the rain, and Jack fell in a swollen creek and drowned.

Since then our emotions have ranged from shock and disbelief, to deeper pain and despair than we ever could have imagined, to little glimmers of hope that shine through in unexpected moments, glimmers that our family will not only survive our loss but somehow learn how to thrive again.

The moms standing next to me in the parking lot talked about eighth grade boys and how they always want to wear shorts in the wintertime. They should have been hearing me tell my own stories about Jack heading off to school or the retreat foolishly underdressed. I wanted to share my own eighth-grade boy stories about how fast they grow and how much they eat, but I don't. Can't. Because Jack never made it past age twelve. He will never be in eighth grade with his friends. So I stay silent. And tears flow down my cheeks.

Grievers learn to function within society, and most days we make it appear pretty seamless. We volunteer at school. We go to church. We shop. We stand around in prayer circles. We try to look and act as normal as possible, even though this often takes more energy and strength than we think we have. We do it mainly for others, because we realize people need to feel okay being open and natural around us, so as not to drive us even further apart from the world and into isolation. We are not aliens, though it often feels that way. But we do carry a constant undercurrent of loss, a schism in our brains, which we gradually learn to adapt to. Most days we manage to operate on the level of the here and now, but sometimes the other part leaks out in church parking lots, and that's okay, too.

There must be safe places for us to be able to bring the loss to the forefront, to open the pressure valve of pain a little bit, without worrying about seeming completely hopeless or obsessive. I remember when Tim and I walked into our first meeting for bereaved parents just two weeks after the accident. We came out depressed and depleted. You see, we were still in a state of shock about Jack's sudden death, but also a state of being tenderly held up by the spirit of God. We went in seeking hope and meaning in Jack's death, and we were earnest in our desire to "be okay!" for Jack's sake and ours. To see parents who were still suffering greatly many years after their children died gave us a window into a despair we didn't want to see. It was too much for us. We convinced ourselves, "Surely we will feel better than they do at five years out!"

I didn't realize then that the meeting was those parents' safe place. We all need safe places. Writing about Jack and spending time with a few friends who are still willing to talk about him and say his name are my safe places. I now know that the grieving parents' pain and desire to continue to tell their stories didn't mean they weren't functioning in society, holding jobs, and taking care of the other members of their families. It just meant that in the day in and day out of living with and adapting to the two-track existence of life and loss, those meetings were one place to openly talk about the one track that is less visible, but still very present.

I wonder if people who read my writing worry that I'm obsessed with Jack and his death. It would be natural to think that, and I too have wondered the same thing about others who have loved and lost. It's a natural concern. We want our friends to get better. We want them to heal and thrive. We wonder if it's healthy to talk so much about the one who is gone.

When I write about grief, my readers don't see much about Margaret's soccer carpool and selling Girl Scout cookies and math homework (gah!) and shoe shopping and school projects, and cooking (double gah!), but they are happening daily. I promise.

But in days filled with soccer carpools and Girl Scout cookies and the like, I need a space like no other in which I can do the hard work of grieving that might so easily be swallowed up by those other things or ignored. I need to be able to turn over ideas in my head, hold them up to the light, and examine them. I need to set aside time to consider the meaning in what has happened, to question God, to grieve not only the twelve-year-old son I've lost, but the fourteen-year-old and eighteen-year-old he does not get to be. I can cry out in the missing, the longing, for the boy who should be with me in body, not just in spirit.

In the examining and crying out, in being authentic and shedding a little light on the existence of the second track of life, I'm hoping that someone else can be helped, either in her grief, or in supporting someone else who is grieving. I don't know how that works, through honest tears in a parking lot or through words on a screen or in a book, but I'm just trusting God on this one. And isn't that what this journey of life is about? Learning to trust, even when we can't understand?

Love,
Anna

"I never imagined the question 'How many children do you have?' would become the most difficult question to answer."

—Alexa Bigwarfe

Awkward

By Alexa Bigwarfe

I have always been a bit socially awkward. Not *weird*, just unpolished. I often stick my foot in my mouth, or I blurt out things without thinking. Basically, I have no filter. Oh, and I have a very strange laugh when I'm nervous. Like the day that they told me that my third pregnancy was actually of *twins,* and I laughed like a cross between a hyena and an evil witch laugh for about an hour until the shock wore off.

Since losing an infant, my problem with awkwardness has just grown worse. Now I make others feel awkward, too. It is not intentional. However, I can take the simplest of conversations and make them almost unbearable for the person on the other side.

This is an example of a recent conversation with a woman to whom I had just been introduced:

"Nice to meet you. What do you do?"

Me: "I'm a stay-at-home mom."

"Oh. How many children do you have?"

Me: I pause, and the stranger looks at me like I'm a weirdo because this should be the easiest question I get all day. I shuffle my feet a little and squirm, trying to figure out if I should say three or four. The woman raises her eyebrows and I'm quite certain begins to wonder if I am on heavy medication.

Finally I say, "Well, I have four children, but I really only have three because one lives in heaven."

Pause.

"Oh, I am so sorry for your loss!" she says, or something along those lines, with an expression indicating she feels awkward and wishes she hadn't gone down that road. There is more shuffling of feet, only this time it is her. She looks around as if trying to find someone to save her from this encounter.

Then I feel awkward for making her uncomfortable.

Silence... I usually fill this void with something stupid blurted out, like: "It's okay though, 'cause I drink a lot."

Okay, so now I'm awkward and an alcoholic. Social services will probably be paying a visit soon.

The other night I was starting down a similar path, but luckily my dear friend came to my rescue. We were at a girls' night out, and I made a comment about when the "babies were born." A woman I just met looked at me; her face lit up, and she excitedly asked, "You have twins?"

Oh no. Here we go.

I replied, "I did. I don't anymore." (Where do you go from here?)

She looked at me with a stunned expression, no one said a word, and my friend blurted out, "But at least we have Tiny, and we sure do love her!" And the conversation rapidly changed topics.

These conversations have helped me grow as a person. I have also come to some important realizations about our culture. Rather than embracing a grieving mother, often we silence her. Rather than acknowledge a loss that will impact her for the rest of her life, we tell her to move on, to get over it, to (God forbid anyone ever say this to me) *just have another one.*

Since I have started writing about loss and the importance of a mother having the opportunity to grieve her loss, whether she was four weeks pregnant or lost a forty-year-old son, I have had numerous women come forward and share with me their stories of early loss. Babies they were afraid to tell anyone about, because of the hurtful reaction from some people. But this child was still their *baby.* And the baby represented a future that will never come to fruition.

I understand the topic of death and loss does make many people uneasy. Especially strangers. I am not trying to make you feel awkward.

I am more than okay talking about Kathryn. I want to remember and honor her, so it does not make me feel uncomfortable to talk about her. So you shouldn't feel uncomfortable talking about her, either.

Hugs,
Alexa

"When I lost my baby at fifteen weeks and was bemoaning to someone about the fact that the hospital pushed off the D & C yet again (the complaining was really just me grieving), the 'friend' shut me down and told me that other people have it worse. Her demeanor was very harsh. I am still hurt."

—Anonymous submission

Survival Tip #12: Try not to take it personally when friends and loved ones disappoint and even hurt you; they do not always understand.

We've already discussed the hurtful things that people can say, unintentionally or not, but these words and actions of the people around us can have long lasting impacts on your relationships. Another contributor was told by her very best friend (not anymore) to just "get over it."

Maybe this tip will help you feel better about any upsetting actions or words that have been done/said to you, and maybe it will help others consider how they approach a grieving mother.

Here are some examples our group shared. We decided to keep all of these anonymous:

- "I have several friends and family who have yet to even *acknowledge* that we lost a baby. Not one word. That is more painful than some of the inconsiderate things that were said. At least those people were trying!"

- "I haven't talked to my best friend since the baby died. I guess she didn't know what to say, so she didn't say anything at all."

- "I have found people have a really hard time when things go wrong. I let go of some friendships when I was going through my losses and really saw a change in people as our daughter's issues got more and more complicated. I think it hits too close to home for some people. I think that is what changes you: the realization that the worse can happen to you. All of a sudden, so many of the little things that people get so bent out of shape about don't seem so big anymore. Deep down I know it's not their fault, but it doesn't make it any easier."

- "I think I got the harshest comment from someone who'd also been through a miscarriage, which really shook me, as I know she'd been really upset about hers, and I'd supported her at the time (when she finally told me). She turned to me and bluntly said, 'Well, you didn't take a pregnancy test and get a positive result—it could have been nothing.' Took a while to get over that one."

- "My younger siblings all but ignored it. My youngest sister, over time, actually managed to make parts of it about her."

- "My sister got pregnant right after my miscarriage, and while I was so happy for her (we had all been waiting), the timing was hard. And another woman at church patted my belly, and when I told her the news, she said awkwardly, "Oh...otherwise, how are things?" I just shrugged my shoulders, my face twisted. But she was just really caught off guard because later when they announced my husband and I were going to fast (for a different reason), she thought it was for the baby, and she came up to us afterward and said that she and her husband were going to fast with us. So she really didn't mean to be insensitive."

And so forth...

Chapter 7: Don't Forget the Dads

Many grieving parents struggle in their relationships. The loss of a baby or child places such stresses on a marriage. In our experience, men and women do not often grieve the same way or communicate well about their loss. My husband and I struggled greatly in the first year after the death of our baby, largely because we went about our grieving process in completely different manners and lost sight of the other person's needs.

This chapter is focused on helping us understand the "other sides" perspective, first with a poem from Dana W. that she wrote to her husband to help explain her grieving process, followed by an interview with Sean Hanish, executive director and producer of a movie about stillbirth, *Return to Zero*, and three contributions by grieving fathers.

To Ken
I want to tell you how I feel,
But I know you don't want to deal,
With hearing me go on and on,
About our baby whose life is gone.

I am scared to tell you that
I'm changed to my core,
And that I know a piece of me
Will forever be no more.

I wish I could tell you I'm 100 percent all right,
And that I don't think about
Our loss every day and night.

But the truth is I think about what we've been through all the time,
It's constantly there,
On top of my mind.

It doesn't mean I'm falling apart,
Rather, instead, it's allowing me, silently,
To pour out my heart.

Our baby was real and a huge part of me,
And it is impossible to think I can just let what happened "be."

It's been so hard masking my feelings away,
In an effort to make you think I'm perfectly okay.

But I don't want to keep throwing my pain in your face
Especially when you are in a different emotional place.

So I keep what I'm feeling hidden away from you,
As I don't want to impose on your heartbreak too.

But it is important you know I'm changed in ways I've yet to comprehend,
And I need your love and support, to help me continue to mend.

—Dana Weinstein

Survival Tip #13: Recognize that men grieve differently, but they still grieve.

Interview with Sean Hanish

Sean Hanish is the executive producer/director of the film *Return to Zero* a movie about stillbirth and the impact it has on our lives. The movie is based on Sean and his wife's loss of their first child late in the pregnancy.

Thank you so much, Sean, for taking the time to be interviewed for this book. We knew that it would not be complete without the perspective of the father, and the difficulties that can arise in a marriage due to loss. We look forward to seeing the movie *Return to Zero* and helping the world to understand the complicated mess life can become after a pregnancy or infant loss.

You have become one of the few voices for grieving fathers. What resources do you know of that are available to help other grieving fathers?

Sean: I hadn't thought about it like that, but I suppose you're right. There aren't many fathers' voices heard in the loss community, which is understandable but hopefully changing. The best resource I know of is Kelly Farley's book *Grieving Dads: To the Brink and Back*. He has a companion website where dads share stories with each other as well. Other than that, there is another loss dad, Paul De Leon, who writes for *Still Standing Magazine* and comes from a father's perspective. His writing is excellent. I think that's about all I know of right now.

There should be more out there, but we're supposed to be the rock, right? The shoulder to cry on, not supposed to look for a shoulder ourselves. But we need a shoulder sometimes too. We lost our children, and that fact gets lost in the shuffle quite often.

What prompted you to decide to turn your story into the movie *Return to Zero*? Will you tell us a little about the movie?

Sean: I had a gnawing feeling inside ever since we lost our son as I moved from commercial gig to commercial gig. I knew that I was in a unique position being a filmmaker and director and that if I shared our story on the big screen, perhaps people would understand a bit more about what it's like for all of us to go through this very specific type of loss.

I talked with a couple of brilliant screenwriter friends who encouraged me and helped me wrap my mind around what a film about us losing our baby would look like. Then, at a certain point, I had to quit making commercials and focus all of my energy on this project in order to see it come to fruition. It was an incredible risk, but I always had faith that I would see this film to completion and that it needed to be out in the world for people to see, feel, and discuss.

The film is based on the experience that my wife and I went through when we lost our first son, Norbert, at the end of our first pregnancy in 2005. We were shocked when it happened — we had no earthly idea that this was even a possibility in this day and age.

The film follows a couple, us, played by Minnie Driver and Paul Adelstein, who has this emotional and spiritual bomb go off in their otherwise picture-perfect relationship. The rest of the film explores the ways in which they grieve so differently, and how their families, friends, and communities mostly fail to understand their experience...and how this loss tears at the very fiber of their relationship until it unravels. It is only after it dissolves that Minnie finds out she's pregnant again.

That's all I'm going to say right now. I don't want to spoil the ending.

What was the most difficult aspect after your loss?

Sean: The most difficult aspect is that I not only lost a child, but I lost the relationship that my wife and I had which was truly wonderful. We were both changed by the loss, and we aren't the same people we were. Our relationship has changed as well. We're still together and didn't split up like the characters in the film do, and we are so grateful for the two children who are now in our lives, but our relationship — that has never fully recovered, despite the fact that we love each other very much.

If you had one piece of advice to give a newly grieving parent, what would it be?

Sean: Most people won't get it, but don't hate them for it. It's simply because they can't or don't want to "go there."

Take whatever time you need to grieve. Because most people don't get it, they won't necessarily give you the time or space you need, so you have to claim that for yourself.

You'll never be the same person again. But that's not necessarily a bad thing.

That's three pieces of advice. I'm over the limit.

What is the best/most comforting thing anyone did for you or gave to you after your loss?

Sean: A graphic designer touched up the one "good" photo we had of our son, and we have a special place for it in our home.

After the loss, a dear friend came over and saw the picture of Norbert. He's an insightful guy and had read the eulogy my wife and I wrote for the memorial service and was greatly moved by it, but when he saw the picture, his jaw went slack. "He's a little boy." It's only then, when he could see it with his own eyes, that he truly got what we had lost that day. We treasure that photo.

Any other information you'd like to share with grieving parents?

Sean: From my personal experience, I can tell you that reaching out is a good thing. There is a wonderful community of people who are waiting to support you. My wife and I didn't know this loss community existed until after we made the film, which was more than seven years after we lost our son. Now, they are part of our family.

If you want to know where to start, there are literally hundreds of communities online and on Facebook. We have an amazing cross-section of over 12,500 people who like Return to Zero on Facebook — so that might be a good place to start connecting with others. But we are only one of so many groups out there that wants to support those who are going through these losses every single day.

Grief: A Father's Perspective

By William Chippich

My name is William Chippich. I am a father who knows the pain of losing a child, a pain I wish no parent ever has to know. Sadly, too many of us do. I decided to participate in this project for several reasons. First and foremost, it is to help people realize how different it is for a father to go through the loss of a child than it is for the mother. It's a vastly different experience, and I hope I can put it into some sort of perspective for you through my personal experiences. Secondly, I will take any opportunity that I can to make the world aware that my son existed and that his too-short life counted for something. He only got one year and two weeks of life, but I cherish every moment.

This story is sad and hard to take, and the timing and the circumstances seem unusually cruel and unjust, but I hope it helps put things in perspective a bit. I will give you a short version of the story and then talk to you about fathers and grief, and about my grief and how I dealt with it (and didn't). It has been sixteen years since I lost Will, and it is hard to put into words even now.

Part One: The Loss
Sunday, December 21, 1997

My son Will had just turned a year old two weeks earlier. Will was our second child, our second beautiful son. His brother Alex was six then, and the boys worshipped one another. Alex adored the baby, and Will wanted to be into whatever his brother was doing. Will was our quiet, sweet baby. He would very often watch the world with his big eyes and silently take it all in as if he were forming an important opinion that he would share with you later. I greatly regret not being able to see him grow into the man he could become someday.

Will had been fighting the sniffles for a few days and woke up that Sunday with a bit of a fever and was unusually cranky. We managed to get a Sunday appointment with our doctor's office, so we took him in. The doctor examined him and declared that he had a common cold and maybe a mild ear infection. She wrote the normal prescriptions and sent us on our way. A common cold. That's it. That was the diagnosis on Sunday, and by Wednesday, he would be gone.

Will slept a lot on Sunday and was fussy and warm, but still very much himself. He ate and he drank, and the fever seemed to be staying level if not getting better. He even played with his brother a bit. I'm glad they had that time together because I don't think they ever got to play again. Later in the day, I went to visit my grandfather, who had been hospitalized with heart problems for many months. He was not well and on a ventilator.

Monday, December 22, 1997

I got up that day preparing for chaos at my job. I worked for a company that was at the peak of their busiest time of year, and as a manager I knew the day would be long and hard. By lunchtime I had gotten the call that my grandfather was fading quickly and that I should get to the hospital right away. I made it just in time to say farewell before he passed. Most of that day became a blur of sadness and love, comfort and grief, making sure my dad was holding up okay and making sure my grandmother was taken care of. Making arrangements with the family and trying to get through this horrible time. Little did I know how much worse it would get in a very short amount of time.

By the time I got home, I was exhausted, and breaking the news to Alex that his great-grandfather had passed made it that much worse. Will was visibly sicker at this point, and his fever was up a bit. He still ate and drank and smiled, but mostly he slept as his mother and I took turns holding him and looking after him.

Tuesday, December 23, 1997

In one of the great regrets of my life, I agreed to go into work that day, despite having lost my grandfather the day before. I told my boss I would work until just after lunch because I knew how much I was needed. I should have been home with my son...I wasn't. Will's mother left him with her mom (who lived below us in the same house) so that she could take Alex to his school Christmas party; we both thought it would make him feel better and cheer him up. I hadn't slept the night before and was even more exhausted than the previous day. I got home and climbed the stairs and changed my clothes.

Just as I was about to get Will from my mother-in-law, I heard her yelling for me. Will had started wheezing and was unresponsive. As soon as I held him, I knew how serious it was. He could hear me but could not look at me. His eyes were fixed to the right, and he was shaking. I had her call an ambulance as I held him and talked to him. It seemed to take hours for them to arrive, but it was probably less than ten minutes. We got in the ambulance, they put an IV in his tiny arm, and off we went. I can't tell you what questions they asked or how I answered all these years later; all I remember of the ride was being so angry that people wouldn't get out of the way of the ambulance and we had to keep slowing down and stopping. The ride seemed to take just as long as waiting for the ambulance to arrive.

We arrived at the emergency room at Children's Hospital of Pittsburgh, and they rushed into action. Doctors and nurses did what they could to find out what was wrong and help my son. Will's mother had arrived home shortly after the ambulance had been at our house, and she got to the hospital just minutes behind us. When she entered the treatment room, she called out his name and he raised his right hand. That would be the last time I ever saw my son respond. It gives me some small, strange comfort to think that the last thing he heard, the last thing he was aware of, was his mother's voice.

As day stretched into night, there were tests and questions. A flurry of family members stayed with us, determined to see us through and be there for Will. Later on that evening came the diagnosis and the explanation. Will did not have a common cold.

Will had meningitis…and it was bad. He was rapidly getting worse.

The doctors explained that somewhere along the line, his mastoid bone had become infected. The infection kept eating away at the bone until there was practically nothing left. Then the infection spread into the lining around his brain and made it swell, and it was putting pressure on his brain. How our doctor missed it—the mastoid bone infection, the meningitis—I will never know. Day became night, and we set up camp in the waiting room and prayed and held out hope. I don't really know why, but at some point in that long night I knew he was gone. No doctor had to tell me…I felt it. I knew. I went to check on him, and his head was cold. Even with all the meds and a drain put in his skull to relieve the pressure, the blood was cut off. The only things keeping him going were the machines and the medicine. All alone, I found a quiet room, fell to my knees, and wept. I offered God my life for his. I begged, I swore, and I grasped at straws, but in my heart I knew it was done.

Christmas Eve, December 24, 1997

After a difficult conversation at 4:00 a.m. with the doctor treating Will, where he admitted he feared he was brain-dead, as I already suspected, I then had the most difficult conversation of my life when I had to break it to his mother that he was more than likely gone. I needed her to hear it from me…not them. We spent the day awaiting the final tests, breaking the news to our families and trying not to fall apart. They performed one last test, giving him one last chance to show any brain activity at all. There was nothing.

Somewhere in the night, our beautiful baby had drifted away.

We broke the news to his brother and let him see him and hug him and hold his hand and say good-bye. How do you explain all this to a six-year-old? He lost his great-grandfather and his brother in the span of two days. No child should ever have to go through all that he did. Alex is twenty-two now and the proud father of a beautiful three-year-old. I am blessed that he is the good man that he is, despite all that he endured.

After the final tests were done and good-byes were said, we had some difficult decisions to make. It was Christmas Eve, but we both felt that we could not leave him there with only machines to keep his heart beating. We made the decision to turn off the machines and let him be at peace. We wept, the nurses cried, and even the doctor shed tears. After the machines were off and the IV was removed, we held him and talked to him and loved him. There was not a twitch, not a flutter. He was truly gone. I will be eternally grateful for the strength our families gave us and the kindness the hospital staff showed us.

The days that followed were a blur of pain and tears, with family and strangers all sharing in our loss. Those days help keep you busy and help numb the pain. Those days pass quickly.

Part Two: The Grief

As men and women, and particularly as mother and fathers, people fall into certain roles that society sets for us. This might sound archaic and old-fashioned, but it's also the truth. As a father, you feel like you are the protector of your family; you fix things, and you make things better. You have to be the strong one. Be strong for your wife, strong for your kids, strong for the world. Just be strong.

When you lose a child, when you can't protect them, when you can't fix it or make it better, deep down you feel like a failure. You can't play your role or do your job, so all you can do is stay strong and not let anyone see the cracks in your armor. If you fall apart, you are failing again, failing your family and ultimately yourself. Even though all you want to do is collapse in a heap and cry or tear things apart and smash them in anger, you hold it in and you focus on your family. You know if you take care of them, you are doing your job. You are playing your role. It's hard to remember to let someone take care of you.

I can't even begin to tell you how many people told me that I needed to be strong for my wife: "She's going to need you. Stay strong and keep it together for her," or "Make sure you take care of her. She's going to need all your strength." I literally remember thinking, *What about me? Who is worried about me? Who is worried about how I feel? Who is staying strong for me?* At the time, I felt alone in my grief and felt I had to hold it inside. It also caused me to feel a lot of resentment too. I resented that she could grieve as openly as she wanted and I could not. It was not her fault or her doing; it was mostly self-imposed, but as much as I wanted to protect her, I really did come resent her over it. It took years for me to realize and admit it, but it's true.

I cannot pretend to know what a woman goes through when she loses a child. I did not carry Will for 9 months. I did not nourish him, feel him grow inside of me, and give birth to him, but he was certainly a part of me and I loved him, too. I wanted to do as she did. I wanted to lie in bed and cry, and I wanted to stand at his grave and rage to the universe in grief. I felt that I couldn't. I felt that I wasn't allowed. To do so was not being strong, not taking care of my family. If I fell apart, I would be failing them as I did my son. As I failed to keep him safe, failed to fix it, and failed to make it all better. I think a lot of men feel this way. We feel we are simply not allowed to grieve the same way. Strangely enough, I think women come to resent men for this (not showing how they are feeling) when our intention is exactly the opposite.

Let me be perfectly clear and honest in saying that no one ever told me that I couldn't grieve. No one said don't cry or that I had to bury it deep inside, but the role I fell into made me feel that way. Just 10 days after Will died, I was the one who had to go back to work to provide for us. I was the one who had to push it down and soldier on. I was a complete mess, and those days were hard, working, trying to stay busy, and to an extent trying to stay numb. I was dying inside but couldn't let it show, and very few people asked how I was doing. They asked about my wife and they asked about my son, but not me. I guess on the surface, I was holding it together. Inside I was as broken as I could be. It was in the quiet times that my mind would wander and I thought I would go insane. Busy and working equaled good; alone and thinking equaled bad. I didn't share these feelings with anyone because if I let it out at all, I would not have been able to stop it flowing out of me. I held it in for far too many years. As men, that's just how we're built. Like I said earlier…it's hard to remember to let someone take care of you.

I think grief becomes its own living thing. It grows, it changes, and it feeds on you, but it never really goes away. Eventually things get better, you live life, and you move on. Two years later, we had a daughter who quickly became the light of my life. She's now fourteen and a teenager in every sense of the word and still the light of my life. I have my son and my amazing granddaughter, and after a divorce and remarriage, I even have two wonderful step-kids. Life is good, but the grief is still there. It will always be there.

It's now sixteen years later, and there are very few days that I don't think about Will. They are mostly good thoughts, though—his smile, his laugh, a happy memory. But there are still bad days, too. Father's Day will always be hard, and Christmas Eve will always be a mixture of happiness and sorrow. Then there are just days where I feel angry that he got cheated out of so much. Like I said, it will never go away. It does get better, though.

If you are reading this and you have tragically gone through the loss of a child, I hope my story helps in some way. Ladies, I hope this might provide some insight into how your man might be feeling. Reach out to him, let him know it's okay to let it out, hold him, and let him know you love him. Take care of him. Men, help yourself, *step out of your "role,"* and let her.

"You'll never be the same person again. But that's not necessarily a bad thing". Sean Hanish

For Clara

A Eulogy by Her Father, David Webb

The saddest and proudest moments of my life are one and the same. I became a father for the first time on a rainy afternoon in July. All the hope and joy of this day became crushed by five words—"We can't find her heartbeat"—and our lives were forever changed.

Clara Edith Webb was loved and adored from her first moments in this world. I still have the positive pregnancy test that Heather took in Texas. The sheer wash of emotions that a simple chemical test strip can cause is awe-inspiring. We didn't know yet if she would be a boy or a girl, or if she would even stay with us. But she did. She stayed and she was welcomed.

A day has yet to pass where the sight of a baby in a stroller or car seat fails to test my eyes' floodgates, and that time may never come. Though she never held my finger in her tiny hand, we did know each other well.

If this sounds forced, it is only because words to express the death of a baby are nearly impossible to find. The loss is not mine alone. The family I love so dearly, the friends so true, the world itself, has lost a great soul, and is lesser for it.

If there is a God, I will hold her again someday. Until that day, I commit her to the care of those loved ones who have gone before her, and to those who will one day rest here beside her.

Sweetest of dreams, baby girl.

Dads Think Differently

By Eric Bothur

After you lose a baby, one statement you hear a lot is, "Men and women grieve so *differently!*" That is true, but what does it mean? My wife and I experienced this after the second-trimester death of our daughter Naomi, and after the subsequent losses of two more babies, Kyria and Jordan. Our differences threatened to pull us apart at times, but they also made us stronger as a couple, as we each had our strong days and weak days. Here are some of the main differences we found and how they impacted us.

I wanted to move forward. She kept looking back. It wasn't that I wanted to forget our daughter, but I needed to set a goal and move toward it, to get our family back to normal, or as normal as possible. We had a one-year-old daughter to care for. My wife needed to get healthy again. We needed to survive as a family, and we needed to work together to make that happen. My moving forward involved taking care of all the family responsibilities to make life as good as possible.

I didn't even have time to grieve, or at least not in the same way that my wife did. Early on I wondered if I was in denial but realized I wasn't denying, but surviving. It was like being caught in a snowstorm. You can't stop to rest and recuperate until you are in a warm place, safe from the elements outside. My wife had time off from work to recover, but I didn't. With all that was going on and trying to keep my job as normal as possible, it left little time for me. It turned out to be weeks or months later that I could really focus on my needs, when the rest of the family was okay or back to our new normal.

People seemed to care more about how my wife was than about how I was doing. Sure, she was sad, but she was getting healthier every day. She had a multitude of people looking after her or encouraging her. I was caring for my family, but we had so much more in the mix now. Where was the time to do it all? Sleep was often forfeited to take care of the urgent. It was a struggle not to become discouraged or resentful at times. It would have been good to have more people who were focused on standing with me.

I didn't want to keep telling our story. I didn't want to talk constantly about it, which it seemed my wife did. What I longed for was quiet solitude to reflect, to pray, to see, to understand. I needed time and space to make sense of this. This wasn't easy to come by, as there were burial preparations to be made and a funeral to plan and each new person or someone new to the events to update with our story. We attended a couple of support groups together, but I was there to show support for her, not me. Rehearsing our story of loss again and again did nothing for me, while it seemed to bring comfort to her.

I didn't want to talk about our daughter as much, even between the two of us. My wife wanted to keep talking about our little girl, but at times I had to say enough was enough. I needed a break. I didn't want to say as many words, and I also needed to keep my sanity to take care of the family and get my wife healthy again. These are the times that brought a wall between us temporarily, but it wasn't that I didn't care. It was just that I needed to be strong enough, rested enough, focused enough, to get us through this ordeal to where life was more normal, or at least as normal as it ever would be again.

One thing, though, that was the same for us is that this event had changed me forever. I never would look at a human life quite the same. I realized the fragileness of Creation and at the same time the preciousness of it as well. I also realized how difficult it was to get help and assistance to travel this path that I had not chosen. There were resources, but they were hard to find, and bereaved parents need a place to find answers and connections. It was out of these thoughts and many conversations with my wife that Naomi's Circle (www.naomiscircle.org) was born. We wanted a place where parents could find help and wholeness again. And one of the areas we are working to create is a Dads' Corner. Men need to be able to seek answers and find help, but they often do not have as much time to do that and may not even be able to attend meetings or read whole books. Hopefully, Naomi's Circle will offer dads a place to turn and start their journey to wholeness again.

In prophesying about the ministry of Jesus, the prophet Isaiah said, "He has sent me to bind up the brokenhearted,…to comfort all who mourn, and provide for those who grieve in Zion—to bestow on them a crown of beauty instead of ashes, the oil of joy instead of mourning, and a garment of praise instead of a spirit of despair" (Isaiah 61:1-3). Ultimately, it was our faith in Jesus that brought us out of the despair and disbelief to a place of joy and praise. It wasn't easy, but it made us stronger than when we set out on this journey, and it resulted in a ministry that has touched many lives and resulted in meaningful friendships with other couples who understand.

♡

"I wanted to move forward. She kept looking back." -Eric Bothur

Chapter 8: There Is Not Always a Reason Why

Most of us find ourselves questioning and second-guessing every little thing that happened during the pregnancy or the child's life and wondering if we had done something differently, the outcome would be different. I drive myself crazy wondering that if I had been a more proactive patient and listened to my body better, could I have changed the outcome?

We'll never know the answer to these questions. We cannot change the past, but the future is in our hands.

It is so hard to understand the loss of a baby or child. So please don't drive yourself crazy with the whys and the what-ifs?

And there is a positive outlook, if you choose to see the bright side. Even if something is incomprehensible at the time, it may work in your life in different ways to result in really amazing outcomes. I think this book is an example. Our group of writers has already decided, even if no one else ever reads this book, we have really helped ourselves through this process.

> Survival Tip #14: Don't drive yourself
> crazy, trying to find a "reason," because
> some things can never be understood.

In Search of Rainbows

By AnnMarie Gubenko

It never even occurred to me that anything could
be wrong. There couldn't be. We were done with bad
news. We beat infertility and were triumphing over
chronic illnesses. I sat there waiting for the doctor to
do an ultrasound, and the only thing going through
my mind was that I was going to get to see my baby
again. I hadn't seen him since two weeks before, at
my 20-week ultrasound. We didn't exactly get great
news at that appointment. We were told that he had
soft markers for cystic fibrosis (CF) or Down
syndrome.

Both terrified me. My sons Nico and Tommy both
battled CF, and finding out blindsided us both times.
Isabella, Tommy's twin, wasn't even a carrier. She
and Tommy were our miracle babies. After dealing
with three years of infertility, I conceived them
through in-vitro fertilization. At the time, we thought
our biggest trial was the difficulty of growing our
family. While six months pregnant with the twins, we

found out Nico, who only had a nighttime cough, had CF, a life-threatening genetic disease that affects the respiratory and digestive system. I was devastated and fell into a depression that took years of therapy and medication for me to stop blaming myself for giving my kids a fatal disease. It took years to convince myself that the God that I believed in and loved wasn't punishing me for something I had no idea I had done. It took years to trust Him and His plan and to stop hating my body for failing me once again.

As the years went by, our boys were doing remarkably well and were beating all the odds. Dealing with infertility and CF didn't make the desire to grow our family go away, and deciding to have another baby wasn't a decision we took lightly. We had to do in-vitro again, and we had to test the embryos before putting them back in, a process that I was conflicted with doing and was very expensive. It took two very stressful and very emotional times for it to work. When it did, we were elated. Things were finally looking up.

The kids were excited, and for the first time in a long time, I felt happy and hopeful. Life wasn't what I thought it would be, but maybe that was okay. Maybe I needed to trust God's plan, because at that moment, it felt pretty good.

It felt good until I had my 20-week ultrasound. We were told that I had an anterior placenta, so I wouldn't feel the baby kick very often. That was a bummer but not a big deal. Then they said the baby might have Down syndrome or cystic fibrosis, and it sent me into a state of panic and disconnect. I begged

God to please make it be okay, because I could not handle anything else. I didn't want to talk about the baby or names or anything. I just wanted to wait the two weeks and go in and have them tell me the mark was just a shadow and was gone. In the meantime, I became really sick and had to go to the ER. While there, they had trouble finding the baby's heartbeat. I wasn't worried because ten days before, they said that was normal.

Once I was upstairs and the doctor was doing the ultrasound, I had no idea that I was about to be blindsided again. I was in no way (are we ever?) ready to hear, "I'm so sorry, AnnMarie. It appears the baby died a few days ago. Judging by the fluid amount, you were either losing fluid and he died, or he died and stopped producing fluid, because the fluid is very low." All I heard was that it was my fault. *My body failed again.*

I started to cry. I was in complete disbelief that what was happening was happening. I wanted to scream, "Are you freaking kidding me?" I wanted to scream that I hated him and to take his stupid ultrasound machine and shove it and bring one that worked because my baby was alive. He was a miracle and a gift from God. He couldn't be dead. How did he die? What happened? Did I do something? When I prayed to God after the last ultrasound and said I couldn't handle anything else, was this His way of "fixing" it? Because I didn't mean it. I could handle it. I just wanted my baby to be alive.

The events after seemed to slow down and speed up at the same time. The pain in my heart was excruciating. I didn't want to have to tell people. I didn't want to have to say it out loud. It wasn't real if I didn't say it out loud. That night, I had to call the kids and tell them. I wanted them to hear it from me. Tommy was the hardest to tell. I explained how I went in the hospital and they checked the baby and found out that he had died.

"So the baby died?" he asked, sounding like he was trying to take it all in and understand it.

"Yes," I said, not being able to be strong anymore.

"Why are you crying, Mommy?" he asked in disbelief.

"Because it's sad," I said, not knowing what else to say.

"So I am not going to be a big brother anymore?" he asked, and I could hear him holding back his tears.

"No," I said sadly.

"Yeah, that is sad," he replied with a shaky voice.

I felt my heart break in a million pieces. How was I going to be able to help my children get through this when I didn't think I could get through it myself? The next morning, on December 7, 2007, around 10 a.m., I delivered Rocco Joseph.

After I delivered him, I was afraid to hold him because I thought for sure it was possible to die of a broken heart. I sobbed while the doctors did what they had to do, and then they gave us some time alone with him. Leo encouraged me to hold Rocco, and I'm glad I relented. To this day, that was the hardest thing I have ever done. I looked at him, and his face and hands and feet and arms and legs looked perfect. I thought he looked just like Tommy. His stomach was scary because it wasn't fully developed, so I kept him wrapped in the blanket. He was dark, and as I held him and cried, I didn't want to ever let him go. I tried to memorize everything about him.

My family went in and held him, and looking back, it was just the saddest, most unnatural thing I have ever been a part of. We had a mini-baptism in the room, which made me feel a little better, and then everyone left us alone again. I remember kissing his head and feeling how cold he was and telling the nurse she should take him because he was cold. She asked if I was sure and that I could have more time, and I said no. She said she'd take a lot of pictures. I thanked her and gave her the baby. One of my biggest regrets is not holding him longer. I wasn't thinking that I wouldn't ever see him or hold him or touch him again. I was only thinking I didn't want him to be cold. I couldn't keep him alive, but I could make sure he wasn't cold. That's what goes through the mind of someone dealing with intense grief.

Suddenly I was making decisions about burials and funeral homes and looking at blurry pictures of my baby, and I remember pressing the button for the nurse, wanting it to be the "stop" button. I wanted to freeze everything and not make any of those decisions. I wanted to hold him again and take better pictures. The nurse came in and said it was too late. He was already sent down for the autopsy. I was absolutely devastated. What was I thinking, giving him back? Why didn't I hold him while she took the pictures so I could make sure they turned out? Why didn't I understand that once he was gone, he was really gone? I didn't want to go home. I couldn't bear to leave him. Once I left, that was it. I would have to face my kids and life as this person I didn't want to be. I didn't want to be the daughter, friend, neighbor, wife, and mother whose baby died. Every part of my identity was overshadowed with this new identity, and I hated it.

The worst part of losing a baby so late in the pregnancy is that your body doesn't know the baby died. When my milk came in, I lost it. It was the beginning of a postpartum depression that I had not experienced before. Thank God for Leo, my parents, and my sisters for being there for my kids when I couldn't be. They came over any chance they could to help me or make sure I was okay. My neighbor and friend organized meals for us for almost two months. It was the biggest help with something I didn't know I would need at the time, but it ended up being the biggest lifesaver. Another good friend had a bracelet made with Rocco's initials on it. How I treasured that bracelet; it was the only thing I had that I could outwardly show that he existed.

I was having a hard time with the thought of having to bury him, so we decided to cremate him and keep some of his ashes in a ceramic heart with "Rocky" written on it. It was the best decision that I made throughout the whole ordeal, because I felt better having it sit on my nightstand. It felt like a part of him was staying with me always.

On December 23, 2007, my family piled into the house of a priest who had been a family friend of ours since I was little. He said the blessing or whatever priests say when they do a memorial. I didn't really listen. I was screaming in my head that this was all wrong. I was wishing it was a bad dream and willing myself to wake up.

We left there to bury his ashes on a baseball field (named after my dad). Since Nico and Tommy both played baseball, most likely Rocky would have too. It seemed a fitting place for his ashes.

The funny thing about grief is that as bad as you want the world to stop so you can catch your breath, it doesn't. Kids still need to be taken care of, homework needs to get done, treatments need to get done, medicine needs to be taken, and kids need to see that their mom is okay, even if she is not. The kids would leave for school and I'd crawl back into bed. I'd get up a half hour before they would come home and plaster a fake smile on my face until they went to bed and I could crawl back in bed and cry.

I didn't want to be "Sad Mommy." I didn't want my kids to look back and have Rocco dying be a defining moment for them. I didn't want them to say, "My mom was happy, and then the baby died and she was never the same." I tried my hardest to be okay. If they caught me crying, I'd explain that I was okay but just sad for a minute.

Christmas was hard, but on Christmas Eve, when we drove up to our house, we saw about fifty luminaries on our lawn. It was the most beautiful sight I had ever seen. *I cried as I saw how many people were praying and thinking of us, and I watched my kids' faces as they read who they were from.* I had very little faith in anything at that point, and knowing I had all of those people believing *for* me helped me feel at peace for the first time since I went into that ER.

I wanted to get pregnant again as soon as possible. I begged the doctor to not test the embryos. I thought CF was the worst thing that could happen, but I was wrong. There is something worse. I didn't care if the baby had CF; I just wanted a baby. He said he couldn't in good conscience go forward without testing, so we scrounged up more money to do another cycle. I knew it wasn't going to work from the beginning. Emotionally, it was torture. When that didn't work, we thought about donor eggs, but it seemed pretty extreme. I needed to find a way back to happiness without a baby.

I remember thinking of my life as a story and that I was the main character, and though I didn't want this to be a chapter in it, it was; now it was up to me. How would the next part of the story go? How would I find my way out of this storm to the rainbow? I turned back to my faith. I was at a rock-bottom place, and I threw up my hands and said, "It's all yours, God. I can't shoulder all of this anymore. This is not who I want to be, so show me who I am supposed to be."

I heard a few motivational speakers talk about the idea that their lives were not their plans. That hit a nerve with me. They talked about letting Jesus drive the bus instead of us; enjoy the ride without controlling where it is going. I liked that idea. I wanted to know more about surrendering and trusting. I needed to trust Him again and know that there was still good that was going to happen in my life. I stopped praying for a baby and started praying that He would show me what path to take. On days that the pain was horrible, I would pray to help me get through those days, one at a time. Sometimes it was as small as Leo knowing I was struggling and taking the kids for a walk. Other days it was a phone call from a friend, and I'd end up crying to her.

The turning point for me was when I stopped looking at God as a punishing God. I stopped thinking of Him using pain and suffering as a way of teaching us but rather as Him teaching us how to survive it. An uncle of mine helped me to see it not as Leo and me giving our kids a fatal disease or failing at keeping him alive, but instead to see it as giving them a chance for eternal life. Ever since the infertility, I didn't believe that God loved me. That's why I didn't trust Him. It was really believing that He did that helped me pick myself up and know that He had good things in store for me. I just needed to trust Him. It was because I wanted my story to be written differently that I was finally able to see that I could be happy again.

I found my rainbow through the storm. I was going to be okay. A fire was lit under me to go back to teaching, and I started to interview. I found out I was pregnant the day after my dream job called me for an interview. I think it is important to say that my rainbow came before that news. That pregnancy was emotionally hard, but I put my newfound faith to the test, and that was what helped me through it. Nine months later, we had a little girl named Gia. We tell her all the time about the big brother who is an angel in heaven that looks out for all of us, and I truly believe that.

With love,
AnnMarie

Survival Tip #15: If you have to make a choice that sucks, know that just because you have to make it, it does not mean you loved your baby less or suffered any less.

Few can imagine finding themselves in the shoes of a mom who is told that her unborn child is sick. So sick, that should they survive through the pregnancy to birth, they will live and die in a world full of pain.

Parents that make the choice to end a much-wanted pregnancy due to poor prenatal diagnosis make their decisions out of love. They take on an unimaginable pain so their child will not have to suffer a moment of it. None of these parents make this decision lightly. The grief, compounded by the need to come to terms with a reality beyond your worst nightmare, lays the groundwork for a complicated emotional journey.

If you have made this heartbreaking choice, please know you are not alone. Thank you, Dana, for opening your heart and sharing your story.

"We did not want our daughter to exist solely because of machines, where she would never run, laugh, play, or interact with me, her mommy, or her daddy or her brother Nate or her dog Misty. We did not want to bring a child into this world that would only be here in a vegetative state, if at all."

-- Dana Weinstein

When You Have to Make the Hardest Choice

By Dana Weinstein

"The baby you are carrying has multiple brain defects, resulting in several structural abnormalities. The piece that connects the right and left hemispheres is missing and the surface is malformed, as well as severely underdeveloped. Where brain mass and tissue should have grown and been plentiful, only large pockets of empty space and gaping holes exist.

"Your unborn daughter will lack the physical coordination to suck, swallow, feed, walk, talk, or know her environment. She will most likely have ongoing seizures 70 percent of the time. And that is best case scenario. If you carry your baby to term, you will need to have a resuscitation order in place prior to giving birth, as your child will be incapable of living without significant medical assistance. She will most likely seize to death upon delivery without immediate intervention.

"And no amount of surgery, medicine, or physical therapy will be able to reverse, improve, or fix this diagnosis."

These were the words my husband and I were devastatingly told at 31 weeks into my pregnancy in July 2009.

We were in shock and confused—how could a fetal anomaly go undetected despite all the prenatal care I received until so late in my pregnancy? It was nearly impossible to comprehend that my diagnosis couldn't have occurred and was impossible to confirm earlier, especially with the advances of modern medicine.

But the harsh reality is that brain development happens well in to the third trimester, and because of the rarity of our diagnosis, it isn't something routine testing can identify.

Prior to receiving our horrific news, I had been happily pregnant and anxiously awaiting the arrival of our second child. For nearly 8 months, I had been loving my baby in utero, writing in her journal and explaining to our son that he was going to become a big brother. Never, *ever* did I imagine I would need to have an abortion—and certainly not one so late in my pregnancy. After consulting with multiple doctors and genetic counselors, and after carefully weighing our options, we made the heartbreaking decision to terminate the pregnancy.

We did not want our daughter to exist solely because of machines, where she would never run, laugh, play, or interact with me, her mommy, or her daddy or her brother Nate or her dog Misty. We did not want to bring a child into this world that would only be here in a vegetative state, if at all.

As much as we loved and wanted our daughter, we didn't want her existence to be one of constant suffering. Letting our daughter go was the most gut-wrenching, impossibly difficult decision, but we did it to spare her from knowing nothing but agony and misery.

After making our decision, we had to wait a week before the process could begin, due to the extremely limited ability to receive abortion care for cases like mine. Each movement of my baby during that time — movement that for months had brought me such joy — now brought only unbearable heartache. There aren't words strong enough to describe the anguish I went through during those days. Every minute felt like an eternity until I could finally end her pain.

Because of abortion restrictions, I could not receive care in my home state or in a hospital, as no provider at the time performed this practice at my baby's gestational age. I had to travel across the country to a clinic in Colorado, to the only doctor practicing late-term abortion for my stage of pregnancy.

To add insult to injury, my insurance considered my abortion care "out of network" and covered less than 10 percent of the $17,500 upfront medical expense for the procedure, not including an additional $3,000 in travel costs to obtain the care. I was fortunate enough to borrow money from family members to pay for the procedure. And with the help of legal counsel and more than a year of appealing, my insurance company finally agreed to cover the total costs. But the financial stress caused my family unnecessary anxiety during an already heartbreaking, devastating, and frightening time.

The shock of the expense, and fear for what that would have done financially for our family, were incredible blows.

Once in Colorado, I will never forget walking up to the doctor's office and seeing "ABORTION CLINIC" in big, bold letters on the side of the building. Those words seemed exceptionally cruel to me at the time. But I knew instinctively I would not hide behind them. I refused to be fearful or made to feel ashamed.

I carry my daughter's memory with me every day and am incredibly thankful that we could spare her from further pain. My son would not be the lively, outgoing five-year-old he is today had we been forced to carry our baby to term. And my two living daughters would not be here if it weren't for their sister and the fact that I could receive quality termination care.

Love,
Dana W.

Chapter 9: Grieving the Death of a Multiple

The death of a multiple is a whole different beast. Grieving the loss of one baby while celebrating the birth of another presents so many unique challenges. For me, I feel like I am never able to fully grieve Kathryn the way one might when a singleton dies. Partly because I had her twin sister in the NICU who was so small and demanded all of my attention. Largely because of the guilt that I feel when I do start to become sad, because I *still came home with a baby.* What right do I have to grieve when I do not even have empty arms? But that is not fair. It's not fair to you if you feel this way. We've lost a baby, regardless of how many remain. I'm cheated out of all of those wonderful twin moments we dreamed of. My daughter is cheated out of her lifelong best friend. Literally her other half.

There are six contributors who lost one multiple. Marcia lost her baby boy one hour after birth. Jessica and I (Alexa) lost our infant daughters in their second day of life. Wendy and Christina lost one of their twins in utero. And Kathy G. lost her son Joey to cancer when he was five, leaving behind his twin brother. In this chapter, we focus on the grief of losing a multiple before or shortly after birth and share the conflicting emotions associated with life and loss at the same time.

"Mommy, I wish Kathryn was here. We were supposed to have two babies."

—Braedan B, Kathryn's older brother

"A year after my son died, I passed a stream of sunlight coming in through the window; it danced across my face, and fell on my toes. Toes I had painted purple, that lit up in the semi-dark hallway. The warm sun on my face felt like a brush of love from my son, and the purple on my toes let me know that I cared enough to paint them. I was climbing out of this hole, and someday, I'd be okay.

—Starr Bryson

Survival Tip #16: You are allowed to grieve
the loss of a baby, even if you take another
baby home.

The Box

By Marcia Kester Doyle

In my hall closet, there is a box hidden beneath
bath towels and bed sheets. Inside the box are scraps
of memories of a child I never had the chance to
know: a lock of hair, some yellowed snapshots, and
the black-and-white ink print of a foot no larger than
my thumb. There was a time when I needed to open
the box daily to reassure myself that the baby existed,
if only for a brief moment in my arms.

I keep the box on a high shelf crowded between
old baby clothes my children have long since
outgrown and the tattered, smudged drawings from
their early kindergarten days. I seldom think about
the box until it's time to reorganize the clothes to
make room for the clutter of new memories. My hand
brushes across the worn flaps, and I feel the need to
open it again, despite the years that separate me from
that part of my past. It has been stored in the closet
for two decades, yet every time I see it, I am surprised
by its presence and what it once meant to me: the
hopes and dreams of a young mother carrying twins.
I lift the lid slowly and touch the silky wisp of blond

hair inside. Folded neatly underneath the sympathy cards and letters is a small cotton blanket. My hand automatically smooths the satin edge, and slowly I bring it to my cheek, remembering the softness of the little boy it once held.

I was five months along when I discovered I was having twins. Before I had time to process the incredible news, a somber ultrasound tech conferred quietly with my ob-gyn as they studied the monitor. My intense joy quickly turned to fear and sorrow when the doctor informed me that one twin was gravely ill and would mostly likely die in utero. Every word he spoke chipped away at my heart as I struggled to understand what he was saying in a cloud of disbelief. There was a blockage preventing the baby's kidneys and lungs from forming properly. In 1989 when this occurred, in utero surgery was still a new concept and had not yet been performed on a twin pregnancy due to a risk of the healthier twin's viability. The procedure at that time was far too dangerous; we had no other option but to let nature take its course. With little hope of raising twins, the grieving process began the day we walked out of the doctor's office.

In the weeks that followed, I cried until I was numb. I felt I had sacrificed one baby's life for another; a decision I had difficulty coming to terms with.

I was put on strict bed rest for the duration of the pregnancy with weekly ultrasounds to monitor the condition of the healthy twin. At each visit, I stared at the monitor and wept at the sight of twin moons floating in a sea of amniotic fluid. And each week my doctor confirmed my suspicions that the unhealthy baby was still alive, despite all odds and the assumption that he would die in utero. There were some days when I wished the ordeal was over so that I could end my baby's suffering and focus on the healthy twin growing inside me. Other days I prayed for a miracle and entertained fantasies of delivering two healthy babies. I tried to ignore what was happening inside my body, as if denying the problem would make it disappear. But ignoring the unhealthy baby was impossible. The bonding process began after conception and was intensified the day I saw two babies on the ultrasound. I felt them moving inside me, and I grieved daily for the one I knew I had to lose.

The last four months of my pregnancy were the most difficult. While other pregnant women were organizing their baby showers, I was making funeral plans. Rather than the happy anticipation of giving birth, *I dreaded my delivery date, where giving birth to one baby meant losing the other.*

I thought I was ready to face the inevitable, but nothing could have prepared me for the gamut of emotions I experienced on the delivery day. Our son died in my husband's arms an hour after birth. We wept for the child we would never have the opportunity to know. Holding him, I lost all sense of time. I remember staring out the window at the stark blue sky and thinking he'd never know the coolness of grass under his bare toes at the park; he'd never know the sticky sweetness of an ice-cream cone in July or feel my heartbeat next to his as I cradled him in my arms and read our favorite bedtime stories. My son knew nothing but the antiseptic environment of the hospital walls that surrounded him.

My healing process was slow, a mixture of joy for the healthy baby I brought home and grief for the son who was buried in a nearby cemetery. Not only had I lost a baby but also the stigma associated with being the mother of twins. There would be no double strollers, matching outfits, or twin birthday celebrations.

Family and friends were eager to help me through the grieving process, but after several months had passed, *they began to put a timetable on my grief.* The general consensus was that I needed to "get over" Jason's death and concentrate more on the joy of having a healthy daughter at home. Well-intentioned comments, such as "It was for the best — raising twins would have been such a burden," and "You lost one twin, but at least you still have the other one to make up for it," were meant to minimize my grief, when in fact they compounded the conflicting emotions I already felt.

As grateful as I was for the blessing of having my daughter, I was equally saddened by the false concept people had that somehow one twin substituted the loss of the other. *What no one understands in the situation of losing a twin is that the survivor is a constant reminder of the one who is missing.* When my daughter took her first step, I cried for the miracle of having her and wept for the little boy I would never see walk. On her first birthday, I looked at the small white cake I had baked and thought there should be two.

My husband and I felt isolated in our grief until we joined a special bereavement group for miscarriage and infant loss. I felt as if I had finally come home after a long and painful journey. At the meetings I could weep for the boy I'd lost without feeling self-conscious about the daughter who had survived. They understood. We gave one another the hope and assurance that we were not alone.

And in time, we healed. We were able to let go of the grief, but not the memory of the boy we loved.

It was once very painful to open Jason's box. It forced me to face a loss I never understood. Today, it represents more than that; it reminds me of the courage it took to work through the loss — something I never could have accomplished without the love of my husband, my children, and the power of faith. The box became a part of the healing process in my grief. Every time I sifted through its contents, I became stronger.

I'll never forget Jason or the softness of his skin. Although our time together was brief, he taught me some valuable lessons. Our children are a blessing, and the special moments we share with them are the little miracles in our lives that make up the memories we carry in our hearts when we grow old.

Jason

Your voice is hidden in the hum
of a respirator, each breath
the weight of a stone
in this sterile room
where shadows of infants
drift across hospital walls
leaves that break loose
from summer trees
scatter into fall

Clouds shift in your eyes
the hard blue of summer
the sorrow of lullabies
you will never know
only my hand against the pale moon
of your face
spirit lifting from my fingers
into the light
your small shadow etched
into the darkening sky.

Lovingly,
Marcia Kester Doyle

Will I Ever Be Content?

By Alexa Bigwarfe

I often struggle with a balance between happiness, sadness, and guilt. *I miss my baby girl so, so much.*

I have *so very much to be thankful for*, yet I am not content. My surviving twin is happy and healthy, and I have two other amazing children. But, selfishly, I want FOUR children. Not three here and one in heaven. I want four children to hug and kiss and screw up in the way that only parents can.

Two days were not enough for me.

But, those two days also gave me peace and more closure. Does that make me a horrible, selfish person that I would have rather had my baby here for two days, even if she was suffering? I always believed they could FIX her if she made it through delivery; they could not. Her life would not have been good if she had survived. I believe that she is better off in heaven. But I still cannot be content.

I kept a daily diary for the twelve weeks that our other twin spent in the NICU. At eight weeks old, she finally broke the 5-pound threshold, was eating decently, even if mostly via tube, had no breathing help, and had been taken off all medicines. We finally could breathe more easily that she would eventually come home. During that time frame, I wrote in my journal, "I wish I could still have Kathryn here too, but I know life would have been so hard for her. My poor girls and the struggles they have faced." Even though I can tell myself rationally that out of the outcomes possible at the time, this was the better outcome for everyone, including Kathryn, my heart cannot comprehend that.

Life often deals us blows that we do not understand and have a difficult time overcoming. I try to put on my happy face day in and day out, but inside I'm a mess. I want to be content. I should be content. And yet I am not.

The pain gets easier over time, as all loss and wounds tend to slowly fade away. But it is never gone. I am constantly reminded that I should be chasing around two toddlers. I constantly wonder what her personality would have been like. I am sad for Charis, who never will have the opportunity to share the experiences that identical twins should have. And then I feel so guilty that I am sad and not content when so many others have no baby at all to hold in their arms.

But I want to tell you mothers who have lost a multiple: You are allowed to grieve that baby, as hard and as long as you want. That baby was a loss just like any other, and it does not matter that you have other children. Nothing can replace that loss. So never feel guilty about grieving when you still came home without empty arms, and I will try to follow my own advice.

With love,
Alexa

Chapter 10: It Gets Better... Easier... Eventually

Although your grief will come and go throughout your life, there will be a time that is not as difficult now. You will find your new normal. Life does go on, whether we want it to or not.

Survival Tip #17: Open yourself up to allowing time to heal you; it does get easier.

The After

By Jessica Watson

I remember rock bottom as a specific moment, a falling deep into the hole opened up the day my daughter left us.

After a hot shower, with my hand over the space she once had grown, I walked from the steam and felt the emptiness pushing down on my chest, my ribs, my heart. I said something normal, something mundane. "Is the dishwasher still running? Should I do another load of whites?" The exact phrase I don't remember; I just remember I did not finish it. My voice cracked, and searing pain closed over my throat. I cried as I sunk to the floor. Rushing to see what was wrong, my husband helped me to stand as I heaved sobs into his chest. He thought I was hurt, and I was; the crack within my heart had broken me wide open. At one point I managed to choke out that I couldn't do this, I couldn't survive. I was furious at my husband when he told me I had to, that I didn't have a choice.

The days and months and years upon years ahead without my child were all I could think about, and at that moment I couldn't imagine surviving them. I wasn't sure how I would make it past dinner or down the hall. My memories of that day are of crying and stomping, screaming and shaking. I don't remember getting up, but I did.

When my grief was new, I spent a lot of time connecting with moms who had lost children before me. Hoping to gleam even a hint of how they survived this grief, I hung on their every word. They all said something similar, that life would get easier and before I knew it the pain wouldn't hurt quite so bad. I didn't believe them, and I didn't really want to, either. Somehow the raw pain of losing Hadley kept her close and reminded me that she had just been here, in my arms, blinking up at me as her chest rose and fell.

Years and years of birthdays and anniversaries have passed since I began my climb from rock bottom. My husband was right; I would survive because I had to. I am now that other mom, the one who can say you will get up again. I can't tell you how or when, but I can tell you that you will. We have lived so much longer without my sweet daughter than with, yet her short days have shaped my every single one.

I am finally in the place of the grieving moms before me who pulled me through, who promised that someday anguish would not muffle every breath. Who told me to put one foot in front of the other and be gentle with myself, and I really truly would survive.

But I am also anchored in an understanding that I am forever changed. I often wonder if I should be doing "better" or hurting less, and I truly don't know. I don't know because there is no map or book or plan for losing a child; there is no story that mirrors your own, with a mother on the other side telling you how she is getting out of bed and staying present and remembering silly things like shutting the car door or signing school permission slips.

Somehow I have survived and put one foot in front of the other, but I have not forgotten. The grief of losing our daughter has traced my every step.

My days are now spent watching my living children grow, settling into the knowing what we truly are missing. I tilt my head toward a daughter who should have a sister the same age. I sigh at the thought she might always be a little bit of a lost soul as she wanders for someone to play dress up and tea party with. She is missing a piece, too. She feels it already. Sometimes I find myself answering questions my children shouldn't have to ask about death and wondering if I gave the right answer to where their sister is right now, how we can talk to her in our hearts and what star she is on, and why she can't come to their brother's birthday party. And sometimes they have the answers before I can speak, her memory following them as they grow.

I am in the place of being as fragile as I am tough, as whole as I am empty, and as lost as I am sure of exactly where my feet are planted.

As much as I would like to crawl back in time and change the *before*, shift the outcome, and continue the whirlwind of caring for three babies at once, I would not change the *after*.

In the moments quiet enough for a conversation from my heart to my daughter's, I tell her how deeply I miss her, how much I wish she were here, twirling in dresses and sassing me at bedtime, and I thank her. I thank her for making me the mother I am, the person I have become.

When she left this world, she pressed a deep gratitude for every breathing moment into my empty arms. I thought I fully understood the gift of life *before*, but I didn't, not until it was taken away. To feel your child breathe in one moment and not out the next is petrifying and gut-wrenching and heart-opening. I have never looked at my children the same again. Each day they wake up is a gift. Every smile, whine, giggle, and tantrum — the whole mess of it — comes in the most fragile package I could have ever been handed.

Most importantly, I am finally in a place of being able to tell that mother who was once me, who could not imagine the years stretched before her that she, you, I, will be okay. We will survive, and we will come out the other side uprooted, bruised, and dizzied but so unbelievably strong that we will forever step with purpose and an understanding of life we could never have found without someone leaving our arms and leading us to it.

With love,
Jessica

"It won't always hurt this bad. The hurt never goes away, but the intensity changes."

—Ann Marie Gubenko

"If you need to surround yourself with others to quiet the noise in your head or fill the space in your heart, do it. If you need to put yourself in a bubble to protect yourself from well-intentioned but potentially hurtful comments, do it. Honor yourself, your needs, and your own process."

—Stephanie Sprenger

It Gets "Different"

By Starr Bryson

My worst nightmare came to fruition fifteen years ago when I lost my tiny, beautiful, and perfect son. He was with me for such a brief time, but he had all of my heart. Only months after I buried my grandmother, I was at another funeral. This time it was to bury my baby. I will never forget the devastating grief. I thought I would die. I wanted to die. I will never forget the crushing guilt. What could I have done differently? Could I have saved him? I'll never forget how helpless I felt. How angry I felt. I was pissed off. It wasn't fair, and I had no idea what to do with all the pain I had in my heart. I didn't want it inside of me; it was too much, too big. There was too much pain and I wanted it out, but I didn't know what to do.

No matter how hard I cried, those shards of pain would not leave my heart. No matter how much I screamed, the ache would not leave my soul. I wanted to throw myself into his grave. I wanted to lie down on the ground and give up, just go over with him.

I wanted him back.

That first night after he passed, I lay in bed, sobbing all night. "Please give him back," I screamed over and over again to an unforgiving, unfair, cruel world. I pretended I'd wake up in the morning and find him in his crib. After the funeral, it was final, and I couldn't hide from it. I couldn't pretend. I had to go on with life without my son.

But how? How do you bury your child — something that is so against the natural cycle of life — and go on with your life? How do you bury your heart and soul with a child and continue to live? How do you get up every morning when your heart doesn't want to beat?

I was barely twenty years old, living in a state twenty-two hundred miles away from my family; my husband was in the military, and soon he was gone, too. It was best that he left, as all we did was fight, and I knew deep down inside **he blamed me**. I could see it in his eyes when he looked at me. He blamed me. And I hated him for that. I hated him.

I was literally alone. Any friends I had made in my short time in this new state before my tragedy avoided me like the plague. There were no phone calls to offer condolences. There were no visits from well-meaning friends, bringing food I wouldn't eat, words that would fall on my deaf ears, hugs that would only start my sobbing anew. I was a pariah.

No one wanted anything to do with me. Perhaps it was because they didn't know how, or what, to do. I understand that now, all these years later. Tragedies are a funny thing sometimes. They can bring people together, or pull them apart.

I was also alone figuratively. Fifteen years ago, the Internet wasn't what it is today. I didn't have the wonderful support system of bloggers, FB friends, or Twitter buddies. There were no support groups, writing groups, or other Mommies of Angels looking for support.

I was all alone in my grief, and I was shunned.

I took to my bed, and I didn't move for months.

I took to the bottle, and I drank too much.

Finally, I did drag myself from the bed. I stumbled to the computer with my bottle and wrote it all out. Every bit of my pain. Every bit of my horrible aching sadness; every lonely moment. It all became words on a screen that I couldn't see through my tears.

I lost nearly a year of my life. Between falling into a deep depression, becoming an agoraphobic hermit, and the drinking, I lost nearly all of 1999.

The day I began living again was profound. I awoke in my bed just like every other morning for all of those long months, with a heavy weight on my chest, a hangover, and no desire to live. No will to move, tend to personal hygiene, or even move.

As I lay there feeling sorry for myself, the familiar tears streamed down my face. I cursed a world that would take my son from me. A world that would forsake me and leave me alone, floundering for purchase in a place that didn't make sense anymore.

I cried that morning, but not all of the tears were for my baby. I felt sorry for myself. I didn't want to be alone anymore; I wanted someone to hold me, to tell me it would be all right. If not now, someday. Someday it would be all right again.

I wanted someone to tell me everything happens for a reason. That he was in a better place.

I craved all of those well-meaning words that never mean anything to a grieving parent. But I had not heard them. I wanted to hear them. And as I laid there in self-pity, sobbing out my isolated grief, a revelation came from somewhere outside of myself. Like a freight train, it slammed into me.

What the hell was I doing?

Would my son want me to lie in bed all day, drinking my life away? Forgetting to eat, not remembering to shower, just wasting away in desperate loneliness?

I was ashamed. I was so deeply ashamed of myself.

My son would want me to live life to its fullest. He would want his mommy to make something of herself. To live enough for both of us.

I had to live enough for both of us.

That morning, I climbed out of the bed and stumbled to the shower to wash away the vestiges of the previous night's hangover. With shaking hands, I put on the nicest clothes I'd worn since the funeral. I trembled, but I applied makeup and blew my hair dry. For the first time in nearly a year, I put shoes on my feet.

I drove to the store and bought food; sustenance for my healing body. I bought new makeup, and I bought new clothes. I worried I was replacing one crutch with another, but I assured myself this would the first, and last, shopping spree in my grief.

Everything I bought was black. Because even if I was ready to get out of bed, to look halfway decent and not smell like a wino with body odor, I was still grieving, and I knew I would be for a long, long time. I wanted to wear black until I was done. It made me feel better. When I returned home, I cooked, and ate, a real meal for the first since I could remember.

And I wrote. I wrote and I wrote for months. I was published in many anthologies and magazines.

Then one day, I realized I was done. I had no more poetry or prose; there were no more words inside of me concerning the death of my son.

It still hurt. Oh God, did it still hurt. I would never be done grieving for that beautiful baby boy. But the sieve was empty, the well was dry, and I had no more words inside of me that needed an outlet. I had written out the very last ounce of pain I had trapped inside my heart; I had cried the last tear onto a keyboard I would cry for him, and again, it was time to move on.

I got a job outside of the house. My writing was put on hold for nearly ten years. Whenever I tried to return to writing, it reminded me of that time in my life when my son had died and left me alone. Writing was all I had. Every time I tried to write, it all came back, crashing in on me. I just couldn't.

I couldn't.

So I worked out in the real world, and I started to introduce colors into my wardrobe. I made new friends, friends that weren't around when I lost my son, friends who didn't think I was a pariah. I traveled that broken and beaten path of grief and pain, and I made it out to the other side.

Here's the beautiful part. It does get easier. The wounds never heal. Time does not heal all wounds; it just gives us a way to separate the immediate intense grief of loss and the pain we carry for the rest our lives.

It gets different.

You realize one day, you can talk about it without sobbing. You can look at pictures wistfully instead of a need to rip your heart out of your chest just to end the pain.

I am no longer the woman who visited her son's grave on the one-year anniversary that screamed and howled like a wild animal. I am no longer the woman who tore up the grass and sobbed and beat the headstone with her fists until they were bloody and bruised.

I am now the mother who cries when she thinks about her son, who tears up when she talks about him. But I can talk about him. And that's beautiful, because I would never want him to be forgotten. He was. He is. He will always be in my heart, and to not speak of him would erase him.

I can write about my loss, and hopefully I can reach someone else. If I can reach just one woman, one lost and floundering soul who feels like she's alone in her grief, then it's worth it to bleed on this keyboard.

You are not alone. There are many of us in this elite club we didn't sign up for and never wanted to a member of.

We're here. You are not alone.

Don't give up. Don't turn to the bed or the bottle, or hole yourself up. Reach out; we'll take your hand. Right now, you may not be all right, but you will be. I promise.

Hugs,
Starr

Survival Tip #18: Find a way to handle your grief.

Grief: Handle with Care

By Heather O'Brien Webb

In the weeks after our baby daughter Clara was born still at 42 weeks and 3 days' gestation, I received a surprising amount of messages from friends and family. There were many beautiful sentiments, but one e-mail, from my good friend Kelly, has stayed with me more than any other, over the many months since July 2012.

In that message, she told me that one way to deal with loss is to find a backpack for your grief. The idea is that when your grief is fresh and new, your arms are piled with so many things — such as funeral or memorial plans, burial or cremation issues, sharing the sad news with loved ones and well-meaning strangers, or even the immediate needs like getting out of bed — and you just can't carry them all.

The smallest things will trigger your grief and cause you to drop all of these things everywhere. It's a constant emotional mess to clean up, and it will overwhelm you.

You pick up a thin, plastic grocery bag and put some of your grief into it. It works temporarily, but over time, as you add new things that you have to deal with and want to remember, it gets heavy and begins to cut into your fingers. You worry that the bag will burst its seams, and you stay on guard, always waiting for the moment when you will have to clean up the contents of your grief again.

Time goes on, and you invest in a pocketbook, and then a duffel bag. Most of your grief fits into the duffel bag, so you only have a few things to balance in your arms, but every time you need to find a certain picture, to feel that tiny locket of hair, to find your baby's certificate of stillbirth or the memorial blanket that the hospital gave you, or to relive the memory of the way their tiny kicks felt in your belly, you have to fumble through the mess in the bottom of the bag to find it.

Your grief is a disorganized mess, and although it is now mostly contained, it still feels overwhelming and all-encompassing. You wonder if you will ever make sense of what your life and emotions have become.

Time doesn't give us back what we have lost, but as it goes by, it does provide us with better means of containing our grief. Now, nearly fifteen months since our baby girl died, I have a large, sturdy backpack with many zippered pockets. It does not contain every bit of my grief, and it is not foolproof. I still find myself forgetting to zip it on some days, and things fall out everywhere, demanding that I deal with the mess immediately. There are still days when I find myself sitting on the floor, lost in the contents of my grief.

One day I may need to upgrade my backpack to something even larger and better organized, but for now, I can keep most of my memories and treasures neatly tucked away, and I only pull them out when I choose to. The backpack gives me the freedom to use my arms for taking care of my family's needs, hugging the people I love, and helping those who have not yet found a way to carry their grief.

Sincerely,
Heather

"Find your life raft, the thing that will keep you going."
—Sheila Quirke

Life and Death

By Sheila Quirke

When I was in my early twenties, I remember wanting my life's work to matter. I had spent my time out of college selling pantyhose, answering phones, and typing legal documents. None of it mattered, and I wanted more. I used to call it "real life," but essentially, it came to mean life and death; I wanted to focus on something that really mattered to people, that made a difference, and that brought comfort.

Fast-forward to a graduate degree in clinical social work and my chosen field, working with older adults and their children, helping them cope with mortality, death and dying, hospice care, and grief. Yep, I was living my dream, a life's work filled with purpose, meaning, and literal life-and-death situations.

There was tremendous fulfillment in working with families to help them better understand end-of-life care, the pros and cons of aggressive medical treatment, and learning when to say when. Memorial services became a sacred and frequent part of my day-to-day work. Caregiver support and bereavement support groups were my specialties.

How do we cope when those we love most, those who are nearest and dearest to us—such as our spouses, our mother, our father—are dying?

I was good at it. Hell, I was great at it.

Fast-forward again to March 2004. I was at the office when I got a call that my mom had suffered what the doctors believed to be a stroke. My dad was en route to be with her, but he was still some time away from the hospital. The ER staff had found my name and number and called me. I got to speak with my mom, but all she could say was, "Okay, okay, okay, okay, okay," except it was perfectly clear from her voice that nothing was okay.

Nothing would ever be the same, actually, because on that day in March, the Ides of March, in fact, I moved to Cancerville. My mom would die eleven months later from the most aggressive type of adult brain tumor, glioblastoma multiforme.

In the midst of her illness and helping my dad care for her on a daily basis (and this was the real-deal type of care, including bathing, grooming, dressing, toileting, and feeding, as my mom had lost all function of the right side of her body that scary day in March), my life's priorities changed dramatically. The life and death I was most focused on were no longer just professional, but personal.

I had never been very maternal, and I never felt strong urges to have children. My life in my early 30s was great, with a loving husband and meaningful work. I worried I might be too selfish to properly care for a child. Seeing my mom in her condition, and feeling blessed to be able to care for her, helped me overcome all the fear I had about becoming a mother.

Caring for my mom taught me how very wrong I was. It was my honor, my privilege, to show love through caring for her. I could do it despite the hardships, both physical and emotional. That caregiving for my mom and dad helped me realize I was as ready as I would ever be to parent.

Gratefully, my husband and I got pregnant easily and quickly. Our beautiful daughter Donna, named after my mom who died while I was pregnant, was born in July 2005, a virtual collision of life and death for us. Lordy, did she bring such joy to the family, such healing joy. She was a wonderful baby. We used to say she was considerate of her older rookie parents. Her very existence and just calling her Donna every day provided a great comfort and gift in our grief over losing my mom.

Fast-forward again to March 2007. Our beautiful Donna, at twenty months old, was not quite herself. She was needy and clingy, her appetite was poor, she would have these acute moments of intense fear and screaming, and her walking was unsteady and changing. Something was wrong. Our baby Donna, our joy and light, was diagnosed with her own brain tumor, papillary meningioma, just three years after my mom's diagnosis.

Donna died in October 2009 at four years old.

I have written extensively about our time in Cancerville with Donna, what it is like to care for a child with cancer, and how childhood cancer irrevocably changes families and erases innocence and naivety. This is not a story of caring for a child with cancer. This here is a story of surviving, making room for grief after the death of a child. This is a story about life and death — our life after the death of Donna.

In my four years of grief after Donna's death, though I have said good-bye to my naivety forever, I have welcomed some hard-earned wisdom. Much of what I have learned, I credit to Donna. Her four-year-old little self lived a life of tremendous wisdom and grace. Her lessons, and her life, guide me in my own. I feel grateful every day.

The idea of a guide for grieving parents intrigued me from the moment I heard about it. Having had a professional background in grief and hospice and dying was something of a gift in my own grief. I knew the basics: everything is normal in grief, you never get over it, and other folks basically don't understand it. All of those truisms are even more so in the loss of a child.

But the flip side of that coin is that knowing a lot about grief — academically, at least — is being aware that there are both intellectual and emotional understandings of grief. The last thing I wanted to do after Donna died was seek professional help. It was so very ironic, given that it was my life's work. But there it was.

We never sought professional help after our girl died. We never attended a support group. I cringed every time an envelope came from Donna's hospice, as I could anticipate what was inside before the envelope was even opened. When the scheduled calls came from hospice, I would politely decline to talk.

I was an embarrassment to grief counselors everywhere.

You see, I knew too much. I knew that there is a literal formula, a mandate, on how and when contact is to be made with bereaved families. I knew when the calls and letters were scheduled. That was the problem. None of it felt personal to me; it all felt little more than…required. There were moments in my grief that I felt ashamed for the work I had done.

Who on earth was I to comfort and support a ninety-year-old widower who had lost the love of his life six months earlier? How did I ever think it was my place to coach and support a room full of grieving spouses and adult children on learning to live after the death of one they loved most? I felt a wee bit like a fraud and didn't want any part of the formalized structure of grief support.

Grief is isolating, and in those first few months of my grief over my daughter's death, I felt every bit of that isolation. Not feeling connected to the structured grief resources readily available was just another symptom of my grief. And the key words in that last sentence are "my grief," not my husband's, not my extended family's grief, and not your grief. *My* grief. For you or another, professional help and support may be *exactly* what you need.

In those days, I felt so strongly that I did not want my grief over Donna to get lumped in with other people's grief. The same approach a professional would take with an older widow or a forty-year-old child or a grandmother had no bearing on how to cope with the death of the most beautiful, silly, clever, loving, and sweet four-year-old girl I had ever met, my Donna.

None of it felt personal enough to me, so I didn't seek it out.

What I did do was gravitate toward those who knew and loved my girl. My husband and I shared our grief every day, despite not grieving in the same way. I leaned on the support network that had been created over the thirty-one months of Donna's treatment, both virtual and actual. Our online community at CaringBridge.org had become a lifeline to me. Words were my salve. Writing about Donna and the grief that accompanied her loss was my lifeline.

In the absence of structured support, I knew that I needed to create my own. I could not, would not, run down the rabbit hole. It is so very easy to get lost after the death of a child. So. Very. Easy.

About two months after Donna's death, I have a distinct memory of sitting on the floor, playing with my almost one-year-old boy, Donna's brother. I smiled and said, "Hello, Baby Jay. I'm your mama." For so much of his first year of life, I had been consumed with cancer. I remember thinking how lucky it was that I breastfed him for his first ten months, as that meant so much of his care could only be provided by me. It would have been so easy for our generous and loving family, almost always present, to have taken over his complete care with Donna's many ups and down in her last year of life.

In those moments on the floor, one thing became perfectly clear. Jay deserved no less of a mother than his sister had had. Her dad and I had been present 100 percent of the time each of her days in Cancerville, despite our fear, our terror, our fatigue, our stress, and our constant worries. Why would this beautiful baby boy deserve any less than what his sister enjoyed?

So right there is another thing to remember in your grief, especially your early grief. Find that thing that will keep you above ground; find that life raft. Find something, *anything,* to keep you connected with the larger world. For me, it was a ten-month-old baby. For others, it might be gardening or writing or volunteering, or cooking or activism. Find it, whatever "it" may be. Find it.

Something else that happened in those early months was the formation of our charity that honored Donna's life. I remember at the time that the last thing I wanted was to create a cancer charity. A fellow grieving mom friend and I used to joke that after losing a child, creating a charity and running 5Ks became almost required things. Cancer had taken my mom and daughter from me, my two Donnas. I did not want to give it anything else. Instead, we created a charity, Donna's Good Things, quite by accident, that celebrated the joy that Donna had in life, and her ability to help us connect to hope.

As time has passed and our charity's works and missions have evolved, so has our grief. Four years later, I find myself at a crossroads, yet again, of life and death. Our lessons in grief have revolved around the balance, at time precarious, between life and death. Though Donna's life ended cruelly short, in October 2009, our family life did not end. For better or worse, we have to keep living and keep moving forward. Juggling the living and the dying has been challenging at times.

A couple of years into our charity and my personal activism around pediatric cancer, I made a decision that has served me well. As painful as it can be at times, I need to tend to life rather than death. It can be hard to explain the nuance of this type of choice, so let me give you an example.

Last year *The Huffington Post* ran the serial blog posts I had written the previous year about our daughter's cancer treatment, "Donna's Cancer Story." These were daily posts that were to run for a month. I was thrilled with the national exposure that would be achieved. It was a proud moment both for my writing, and as Donna's mom.

The response was extremely positive, and Huffington Post Live, their online video community, contacted me in late October to invite me to appear as a guest on a panel discussing childhood cancer. Hooray! I was thrilled. And then they mentioned the date and time of the discussion, October 31 at 5 p.m. My elation was quickly deflated. Halloween afternoon at 5 p.m. is prime trick-or-treat time in our neighborhood. My son was heavily anticipating the plans we had made with neighbors to trick-or-treat together. At 5 p.m.

Hence, my choice. I could choose my living child and trick-or-treating — at three years old, his first time to really trick-or-treat with joy — or I could choose my child who had died and the opportunity to advocate against the disease that had taken her from us.

I chose life.
I chose Halloween.
I chose joy.

A wise friend once told me, early in my grief, to "go to the joy." I valued her words, as they held a lot of weight for me. Just a year earlier, she had lost her husband of forty-plus years, her high-school sweetheart, her partner in all things. When someone whose grief carries weight for you gives you advice, listen. I am glad I did. I often choose to go to the joy. I have worked through the guilt associated with that and have come to embrace that my daughter, my sweet Donna, always chose joy. Children do this naturally and instinctively, without guilt.

We have so much to learn from our children. Even in grief.

You may be new in your grief, which is what brought you here. Trust me when I say you will make your own path, entirely different than mine. There is no formula to grief, no set stages that you will pass through, and no magic pill to make it all go away. Your grief will last a lifetime. Like a loyal puppy, it will never leave your side. It is not to be feared or pushed aside. Make room for it, embrace it, feel it, but don't let it define you.

I am a grieving mom. It is part of who I am. I have brown hair and blue eyes, and I grieve. Every day. I am no longer fearful or ashamed of this grief that I carry. It no longer overwhelms me, for the most part. Some days it does, and that is okay. I will take that day and tend to my grief wounds. Acknowledging those wounds that will never fully heal, never go away, is what allows me to keep living.

Life and death is something that I face every day. My youthful career hopes and ambitions and naivety have become more realized than I ever could have imagined. I chuckle at that and wipe away a tear at the same time. Life and death, folks. Life and death.

Xoxo,
Sheila

"We will find the shiniest star and tell her to come home."

—Jessica Watson's daughter, who lost her identical twin sister

Survival Tip #20: Keep the memories alive and honor your child.

There are so many ways to honor your child and remember them that are helpful when dealing with your grief, such as doing the "Walk for Remembrance" or releasing balloons or lanterns, participating in the universal wave of light, and more. The October 15th website and many others (listed in our resources section) provide ideas and suggestions. In the next story, Kathy shares how she remembers her son.

I Won't Cry on the First Day of Kindergarten

By Kathy Glow

I cried when I escorted my oldest son to kindergarten. As I looked around at all the veteran moms rushing in and out of the building, I felt silly and ashamed as I quickly tried to wipe my tears away.

I didn't want them to think I was crying just because my baby was going to kindergarten. For some reason, I wanted them to know that I wasn't one of the moms who was rushing off to a "boo-hoo" breakfast with her friends and lamenting the passing of her child's early days at home.

I wanted them to know I was crying because I never thought I'd ever be taking my son to kindergarten.

And I wasn't entirely sure, once there, he'd even be able to finish the school year.

Ever since Joey was little, he loved school. I remember once, when he was three, he found a backpack and heaved it upon his tiny shoulders.

"Bye, Mommy. I'm going to school!" And as he turned and walked away from me, the huge backpack bobbing underneath his wavy blond head, I surprised myself by tearing up.

I never cried when I took him to preschool, though. He was more than ready by that point. His twin brother, "Slim," had already been in an early childhood special education preschool classroom for six months, and Joey was excited for his turn.

When I found out I was having twin boys, I pictured them walking hand in hand to school, the best of friends. While I was disappointed that they wouldn't be going to preschool together, I was thrilled when our kindergarten of choice accepted them both.

I took picture after picture of Joey and Slim smiling and hugging on Kindergarten Round-Up day. My dream of the boys walking hand in hand to school together was finally coming true, and I was really happy.

But that spring, Joey had been suffering from debilitating headaches so severe that he would vomit. One day, about two weeks after Kindergarten Round-Up, Joey woke up having a grand mal seizure.

In a flash, there was an ambulance ride, a CT scan, and an ER doctor telling me in deadpan, "Bad news, it's a tumor." Every parent's worst nightmare became a reality for me in that moment.

We met with an oncologist. Joey's tumor had a name, anaplastic astrocytoma, and a grade of four—the most severe.

We met with a neurosurgeon. The tumor was inoperable.

We were told our five-year-old son was going to die.

At that moment, any hopes, dreams, and plans I had for Joey began to die along with him.

One of Joey's oncologists wanted us to sign a Do Not Resuscitate (DNR) order for Joey because, in his words, he would "not likely make it through the summer."

So we set about doing all of the things that had been parked on our "someday" list. We visited the beach in Florida, we took the boys to a concert, we went to Disney World, and we enjoyed long weekends at the lake. Mostly, we spent time as a family, making memories and taking pictures and videos of our dying child—for someday. For the days when we would have to help his three younger brothers remember him.

After a summer of chemotherapy and radiation, a summer spent staring at that signed DNR on my desk, Joey and Slim were ready to go to kindergarten.

We walked in to school that day as a family, something even Joey's doctors didn't think would happen. We smiled for a family picture, and escorted Joey and Slim to their kindergarten room. Joey was proud as he put on his nametag and arranged his school supplies at his place on the table.

Day after kindergarten day, Joey would come home and not remember a single thing about his school day. It absolutely broke my heart. This was a child who would tell me every last detail about all two hours and forty-five minutes of his preschool day. The tumor had robbed him of his razor-sharp memory.

He would frequently nap at school and miss most of the school day. By Christmas, he was only going half days. By April, we withdrew him from school. In June, we buried our beautiful six-year-old son.

That summer, our family was heavy with grief. We had turned our backyard into a relaxing oasis with new landscaping, but all we could think about was how much Joey would have enjoyed playing in our new yard.

I fell into a deep depression that not even the antidepressant I was taking could quell. It was difficult for me to get out of bed, and it was even more difficult to take the boys on any fun outings that summer. Everything made me think about Joey — how much I missed him, how unfair it was that he was not with us, how much more fun we would be having with him by our sides.

I talked about him every day. We'd see a yellow car, and that would spark a memory.

"Knox," I'd say to Joey's five-year-old brother, "remember when you were trying to learn your colors, and yellow was hard for you, so Joey made up a game looking for yellow cars?"

When I would see Slim playing with Joey's beloved stuffed cat, Stripey Kitten, I would say, "Remember the time Joey dropped Stripey Kitten in the toilet? We all called her 'Stri-PEE' Kitten and laughed about how it was a good thing there was no poop in the toilet? Then she'd have to be called 'Stri-POO' Kitten?"

Even Lil' C, who was only a year old when Joey got sick, would laugh and beg me to tell him stories about Joey.

And so I did. The time when Joey was a baby and he shot poop across the room (that one always got a laugh). The time Joey and Knox ran streaking around the backyard, playing in the hose. How Joey was a terrible hide-and-seek player because he would sit in his hiding spot and giggle loudly. His creativity when picking out Halloween costumes. That he loved animals and riding his bike and helping Daddy in the garden.

And so our healing began. Even mine. The first year after Joey's death, every milestone brought tears: the first day of first grade, school picture day, holidays, the passing of the seasons, baseball and soccer games, birthday party invitations. These all brought a flood of emotions ranging from sadness, anger, rage, helplessness, self-pity.

But with each experience, we talked about Joey and wondered what he would be doing or thinking. This helped Slim, who was pretty quiet about his feelings, except for having bursts of passionate disagreement when we'd say that Joey was gone.

"He's not gone! He will always be with us in our hearts!" he would declare adamantly.

Talking helped Knox work through his feelings of abandonment over losing his best friend and idol. It made it okay for him to say that he missed Joey or felt sad or wished Joey could be there to see him finally ride his bike without training wheels.

And it gave Lil' C some memories to make of his own. It gave him a connection with stories to tell and a love to keep growing, even though its object was no longer with us.

One year and two weeks after Joey's death, we welcomed another son into our family—an unexpected little gift. He was sweet and perfect and reminded me so much of Joey that I started telling him about Joey right away.

That's the thing about experiences; they turn into memories that you can keep forever and share over and over. Although our new baby, Baby E, will never have known Joey or experienced one of his super-tight big-brother hugs, seen his ability to make any situation fun, been swayed by his happy motivational attitude, or delighted by his amazing creativity, he will get to share in those memories. He is two years old now, and he has heard the same stories that the three older boys have heard. He can pick Joey out in a family picture, and he listens intently when we all talk about him.

When Knox and Lil' C went to kindergarten, I didn't cry. I was excited for them to go. They were healthy, safe, and ready. I knew they would be okay.

I have watched other mothers cry on the first day of school, or get angry over a lost shoe or forgotten backpack. I don't begrudge them those feelings. It's all in what we know. For me, I have had one of the worst things happen to me as a parent. All the rest are merely annoyances that I try to put into perspective, including the sibling squabbles and the forgotten assignments, or wanting to quit Cub Scouts in the middle of the year. Those incidents are not a big deal to me anymore.

As we move ahead in our lives, I try to focus on family, reminding the boys of the blessings we have. Even if it were all gone tomorrow, we would still have each other. And our memories, of course.

If fate allows, our other boys will move ahead in life with graduations and proms and college experiences and friends and sports and activities that Joey never got to experience. I will have no memories of those to share with his brothers. The memories of Joey stop at age six, where he will remain a little boy forever.

It's inevitable that the passage of time will always make me sad, such as seeing Joey's brothers grow up without him, watching his friends (especially the twin brothers he met in preschool) getting older and taller, and knowing that everybody else around us is moving on with their lives.

So I try to keep the memories alive for the boys because I know their own memories will fade with time. I'll keep talking about Joey's likes and dislikes and the sweet, cute, and funny things he did.

We have a new little person who is only two and for whom all the Joey stories will be new. Baby E will have a whole new set of firsts, like the first day of preschool, the first time he rides a bike or goes camping, or the first time he kicks a soccer ball or helps his dad in the garden.

He will have a first day of kindergarten, too. And even though he is my last baby, I don't think I'll cry on that first day. I'll remember all the other first days of kindergarten, especially Joey's, and it will make me smile because at least they all made it there.

And at least it will be another memory to share.

Love and Hugs,
Kathy G.

Survival Tip #21: Let happiness find you again.

A New Happiness

By AnnMarie Gubenko

After Rocco died, I feared that I would never be happy again. How could I smile or laugh when my baby wasn't alive? It felt wrong. It wasn't even a matter of being able to or wanting to for a while. I cried for all the times I took being happy for granted. I longed to feel happy or something besides the intense pain in my heart and feared that it just wasn't ever going to happen.

I always thought Rocco used cardinals to send signs to me. The morning of his memorial, I was so distraught that I sat by the window just staring at the snow coming down. A bright red cardinal landed on a tree branch in front of me and just looked in. I wanted to believe — no, I needed to believe — that it was Rocco telling me it was going to be okay. For the first year, life became a series of timelines. First it was this time a week ago, I found out he died. Then it was this time a month ago, I found out he died. The 7th of every month was like a black cloud of reliving what happened. On every one of those days, I'd see a cardinal at some point. I began to look for it and was relieved each time I'd see one. Seeing a cardinal became my new happy.

I was hard on myself. I would get mad and try and be happy. I'd go out with friends or try and do things that once made me happy. I thought it would be a good idea to go on a girls' vacation, and it was a complete disaster. I thought I could go and morph into someone else. I wanted so badly to feel happy again, so I'd drink, laugh, and be free so that I could for just a short time forget who I was. Then I'd see myself in the mirror and think, *Nope, still there. Still this broken, sad person.* I avoided mirrors after that, which wasn't good because there were pictures where, to me, I was unrecognizable. I thought by going away, I could run away from myself and the sadness that engulfed me, but no matter what I tried to do, I was trapped. It became painfully clear that I could not escape myself.

Happiness continued to elude me. I would be in a situation that I knew should make me happy (birthdays, Mother's Day, Christmas), but even if I attempted to let myself "feel" happy, the stabbing pain of Rocco not being there would hit me like a ton of bricks, and if that didn't do me in, the guilt did. It felt like a betrayal to him. It was as if the only way I could prove I loved him was by being sad. I can't remember a single time in that first year that I felt happy, outside of seeing a cardinal, without the pain or guilt.

Then after a year or so, Tommy, who was seven at the time, asked me if I was always going to be sad. I didn't know what to say. I couldn't look at his little face and lie, but the truth was, I didn't know. I knew one thing, though. I owed it to my kids to not have *their* stories have "Sad Mommy" in them. It wasn't fair to them.

I remember the first time I felt happiness without the sting of guilt. We were in Disney World with five other couples and their kids. I was sitting by the pool with friends, watching Nico, Tommy, and Belle playing in the pool. I started laughing at the kids. They were goofing around and having so much fun that I couldn't help but join in and laugh with them. It felt good to laugh. I didn't immediately think of Rocco. I let myself off the hook later when I thought back to that moment, realizing I didn't. I waited for the guilt to hit as it usually did. How could a mother smile or laugh after she buried her baby? Surely her broken heart wouldn't let her, but the guilt didn't come. It was as if my heart and mind were tired of being sad. That was the first moment of finding happiness again.

It wasn't all gold after that. It was inconsistent, but I learned to deal with the pain that gripped my heart because I knew it wasn't going to last forever. At some point soon, I would laugh again. I'd feel peace again. That helped me weather the worst of the storms. There were days that I went all day without thinking of what I had gone through and what I lost, and then there were days when something would trigger the memories and it would hit me like lightning, and I'd feel the grief all over again.

I'd see cardinals when I was feeling low, and they always made me smile. They would remind me that it was okay to be happy. I believed that he was always with me, letting me know he was okay so I could be okay, too.

I struck a balance with living with the pain and not feeling guilty when I was happy. It wasn't the same happiness as before, and that did make me sad. It was a new happiness that I appreciated more because I knew the other side. It was a happiness built from strength, knowledge, and surviving my heart being shattered and slowly, in time, being put back together.

Hugs,
AnnMarie

"I remember driving home from the NICU one day in February. It was really warm outside, the sun was setting, and the sky was pink. We had learned that day that Charis would have her surgery in one week, and, if all went well, she would be going home in a week. After three months. I felt happiness in that moment. True 'the sun'll come out tomorrow' kind of joy! Even though it was immediately followed by sadness that her twin sister would not be coming home with her."

—Alexa Bigwarfe

Survival Tip #22: Control your own happiness.

Controlling Happiness

By Tova Gold

I remember the moment it first occurred to me that maybe I could control my happiness.

Perhaps that line seems out of place in a book about surviving the loss of your child or baby. Perhaps it is. But I don't believe so. Grief has taught me so many powerful lessons about life and, specifically, the life that I want to live. I want to live a life filled with love and a vibrant, beautiful, and fierce joy and happiness. Grief taught me how, and it is the message I want to share.

I was standing at the foot of my bed. It was about 11 p.m., and I was getting ready to get under the blankets, close my eyes, and hope for a peaceful night's sleep. It had been a pretty good day, considering.

My twins had died a few months prior, and most days had been filled with tears. Twin-to Twin Transfusion Syndrome had stolen their lives when I was 24 weeks pregnant. Darkness, anger, pain, and heartache had become my best friends. I never tried to stop the tears; there seemed no point. When they came, I knew I had to welcome them and let them run their course through me. Sometimes it happened at work. Other times it was on the street, just walking to catch my bus. Sometimes I'd put on my sunglasses and think, *Who do I think I'm kidding?* But I'd wear them anyway and let the tears escape from behind the extra-large lenses, roll down my cheeks, and drip off the bottom of my chin, where I'd wipe them with the sleeve of the unwashed sweater I'd thrown on that morning without thinking or caring.

Grief was my companion. I looked for it in the moments between my life's moments. It filled the blank spaces of my day with its strength and all-encompassing energy. When I heard anything, it was filtered through the ears of grief. *I can't believe she'd say that to me. Doesn't she know I have two dead babies?* were the thoughts that found me, mid-conversation, about something as benign as recipes. When reading something, I'd read it through the eyes of grief, weighing all that is sad or happy against the feelings I felt in grief, about my dead babies, my pain. Watching TV, doing work, having dinner with friends, going on vacations—all of it, *all of it,* filtered through grief.

And so there I stood, at the foot of my bed, getting ready to end my day and file it away as a "pretty good day," and I felt a tug. Something inside me was pulling me away from my bed. Something inside was saying, "It's only eleven o'clock, Tova. Go downstairs. Get on the computer. Go find a reason to cry."

The acknowledgement of that thought shook me. It was almost like an addiction, and I was feeling the need to "feed" my grief. The computer was not a new outlet for me. I'd spent thousands of hours there over the past few months, connecting with the other women who had experienced loss. I'd log onto any one of my many support groups, where I was welcomed with love and understanding, and where I ultimately gained the tools to feel stronger and begin to heal.

But this was different. On that day, I didn't want to go to those sites. On that day, that "pretty good" day, I wanted to go to the sites that would rip open any wounds that may have begun to scab over. I wanted to go to the boards with the moms who were expecting twins in the same month as me, and look at their healthy, beautiful birth pictures. And I wanted to do it to compound my pain.

I began that day to recognize a pattern to the pain and grief. When we let the grief in, which we must do in order to get through it, we get into a habit of maximizing our exposure to it. In grief, our brains open us up to every version of the pain that surrounds us. What we hear, what we see, and what we read—all of that—are taken in through the narrative of grief. We send our minds on journeys that only work to compound the grief even further, playing out those "what-ifs" and "if-only's" in excruciatingly painful detail while we go through our day, sob in the shower, brush our teeth, and stare at a stranger's reflection in the mirror. We go places that remind us of our pain. We write poetry that pulls our pain to the surface so we can explore it further and share it with others and analyze how it makes us feel.

And to do all this is normal, and healthy even.

That pain is an unwelcome permanent visitor in our life, and we need to do this, to bare our souls to this pain, in order to come to a place of peace with it.

That moment, at the foot of my bed, I had a thought. What if, instead of viewing the world through a filter of pain and grief, one made the decision to view it through a filter of love and joy instead? What would happen?

I didn't know. I didn't know if it was possible or how one would even start to explore that idea. What I did know is that I had never, *ever* felt anything as intensely and profoundly as I did my grief. Even the joy of my wedding and the birth of my older daughter were, in retrospect, tempered by the stress and anxiety that go along with those big life events and changes. I wondered if I was even capable of feeling anything with as much purity and consistency as I felt my grief. Once I realized I was capable of feeling *something* in a way that was so honest and all-consuming, I decided it must be possible to recreate that intensity with other emotions.

That was the beginning of my search. It started slowly — very slowly. In many ways, I wonder if I even fully realized I was doing it. I knew in my heart that while I needed to fully honor my grief, my daughters would want me to live a life filled with joy, so I began paying attention to the moments that left me feeling happy, cheerful, and elevated. They were tiny moments, but I allowed them to enter my life without guilt or regret. I no longer stopped myself mid-laugh or mid-smile to check in with my grief. Instead, I marveled in that which had made me feel happy and tried to compound that feeling, make a mental note, and store that positive stimulus away for later, when I needed to find a moment of joy.

It was within this time period that I started to wear sequins. Yes, sequins. I realized that there were moments when I looked at happy, colorful, and sparkly clothes and felt elevated. I'd always been attracted to sparkly stuff like that, but as an adult, I'd stopped paying attention to that simple, superficial love. It just seemed shallow and unimportant in the context of being a "grown-up."

But there I was, in the depths of grief, feeling lightened by the way a plastic little disk sparkled in the sunlight. So I followed that feeling and began sprinkling sparkles into my wardrobe.

I began sharing this sequins obsession in my online support groups. I remember reading from a mom who was approaching the one-year anniversary of her loss and was feeling draped in grief. I suggested she wear sparkles. I hesitated long and hard after writing my comment and before hitting "post." On the one hand, I knew that wearing happy clothing had been helping me tap into a true happiness and strength, and I believed it could help her, too. On the other hand, I recognized that it might sound crazy at best, or insincere and mocking at worst. But I hit "post" anyway, and it was clear from the replies that my intentions were taken in the right way. I was filled with joy and purpose when I started receiving e-mails from women thanking me for making them smile at the sight of sparkles. It felt incredible to be able to share something so random and lighthearted, and yet see that it was actually impacting women on a much deeper and meaningful level. And so, as my quest to find my own joys and compound them grew, I continued to joyfully share my sequins obsession with baby loss moms in private support groups.

And then, one morning, on the bus to work, I read on Facebook the line that changed the course of my life:

"I used to be much more muchier, I think I've lost my Muchness."

By the time I finished reading the sentence, my brain had exploded at the truth of that statement. I'd never known a word for that…that thing. That indescribable part of you that lives in your gut and allows you to express yourself so fully and boldly and *you*. It was *Muchness,* and I was tapping into mine by wearing and sharing my sequins obsession.

I decided that day to truly step into my Muchness. To explore and exploit those "muchy" thoughts in my head and actions, in much the same way the grief had forced me to explore and exploit it. With that in mind, I asked myself if I had enough sequins in my closet to wear them every day for 30 days. I would invite that light into my world every day for 30 days. It would be my 30 Days of Muchness Challenge, and I would photograph and share it on my Facebook wall.

And that is what I did. Every day I started thinking about what "Muchy" clothing item I could wear that day, and then I'd take a picture and post it to my wall. Within the first three days, I noticed something happening. My energy was shifting. People were responding, and my joy was growing. I was feeling elevated and inspired to think about what I would wear or do for my "Muchness" the next day. I was feeling inspired, creative, and excited for each new day and the opportunity to do and share something joyful.

As the days passed, something else happened. I started to take my grief "out of the closet." See, for the first year after our loss, I'd hid my pain. I'd been online, in those private groups, sharing my heart with other baby loss parents, but to the rest of the world, I appeared generally "fine." I kept my pain inside because I didn't want people to think I'd "lost it" and "needed help" to "get over it."

A few months before my Muchness Challenge, we'd passed the one-year anniversary of our loss. As that time drew near, I'd felt the need to honor my daughters. I was 8 months pregnant with my rainbow daughter and felt sad when I realized, upon the joy of her birth, our twins would be all but forgotten. In large part, I believed they already were.

And I couldn't accept that.

I opened up their memory box and pulled out their ultrasound pictures, and started creating a memorial video. I didn't initially plan to send it to anyone, but by the time it was done, I realized I needed to. I needed to send it to all the people that had known I was pregnant so that they did not forget my babies. So that they understood that I had not forgotten them and that my pain was real and continuous, and that my babies were important.

On the first anniversary of their death, I sent that video. I asked my loved ones to acknowledge my daughters' existence.

It was an incredibly healing and strengthening experience.

But it wasn't on Facebook or in a place where strangers could judge me en masse. Yet I knew that sharing my girls was something I yearned to do. So, months later when I began my Muchness Challenge, it was a way to gently let the world know: "I am sad, but I am choosing to celebrate joy. I have been hurt because life is hard, but I am making the decision to look for the light and share it with you. I hope it helps you feel joyful and inspired with me."

The response was amazing. The Muchness Challenge fully transformed the perspective through which I viewed the world. I no longer needed to see the world through a filter of grief. I realized that filter was a habit formed over the days and months of grieving so intensely; it did not need to be permanent. Now I was viewing the world through a filter of joy, light, and color! The 30 days of Muchness searching and creating, and sharing these "Muchness Moments," had truly created new habits and formed new pathways in my brain, pathways that starting compounding and building upon those small moments of light and joy.

At the end of the 30 days, I launched my website, FindingMyMuchness.com. I created it so that others could take their own 30-Day Muchness Challenges, inviting their own light and joy back into their lives one tiny little moment at a time. The site has changed many times over the years. It now offers guided inspiration to help you get to the other side of 30 days and change your perspective, while you document your Muchness journey on social media or your own blog. It's amazing to watch women who are trapped in darkness tap into those tiny moments of light and then work to compound them, celebrate them, and grow them every day for 30 days. And it's not just sparkle. Women have taken the 30-Day Muchness Challenge using everything from cooking and reading to photography and nature as their bouncing-off theme. Whatever it is that sparks them is fuel for the challenge. It has transformed lives. I've seen women trapped in grief for years and years, where the habit of grief, the filter, had become so familiar that they thought it needed to be a part of them. But it doesn't. We just need to create new habits, new filters—ones that ignite our lives and help us celebrate the babies that we were blessed to know, even if it was only for a short time.

My wish for every baby loss parent is that they come to know their strength as a member of this community. That they come to understand that grief is a bittersweet gift. The darkness can coexist with light, and our deepest grief can introduce us to our human capacity to experience our deepest joy.

We cannot control what makes us happy. Those details are written into our DNA at birth. But we can seize onto that which does and nourish it, explore it, celebrate it, and make it a habit. I believe our children would not want you to live out our days in grief. They would want us to celebrate life and the gifts we are given. They'd want us to drink in all the beauty of this world, enough for them and us, a million times over.

In Muchness,
Tova

"The second day after Joey's funeral, his four-year-old brother woke us up by standing beside our bed proclaiming, 'Look, I'm a Transformer!' He was wearing NOTHING but the Transformer mask."

—Kathy Glow

Chapter 11: The Ever After—Helping Others through Our Loss

Grieving mothers have been the catalyst behind incredible organizations to support other grieving mothers and families. Organizations such as Sunshine After the Storm, Inc., Donna's Good Things, Teeny Tears, the Twin to Twin Transfusion Syndrome (TTTS) Support Team, A Little Thunder, Naomi's Circle, Mikayla's Grace, the Carson Project, Mommy to Mommy, Molly Bears, and so many more have been started to provide support, advocacy, providing care packages, and providing love to grieving parents. We have included a resource guide at the end of the book with more information on these and more organizations to help you through this dark time.

♡

"It {my loss} has really helped me to give back. You can start by doing something small, such as donating to an organization, crafting a quilt square, or participating in a walk. You never know where the connections you make at these events might take you."

—Christina S

"I started sewing diapers for Teeny Tears as a way to physically do something to give to others and remember my baby. Since then, we have assisted in building a children's garden in her memory and I have found countless organizations to give my time and energy... for the love of Kathryn."

—Alexa B.

Survival Tip #23: Help others through this
miserable journey; you will find joy and
peace.

Naomi's Circle

By Kristi Bothur

I was in the hospital when I miscarried our
daughter Naomi as a result of a life-threatening
abdominal infection raging in my body. Emergency
surgery followed, and recovery kept me in the
hospital for another week — much longer than the
average hospital stay for a miscarriage or stillbirth.
The floor I was on was the one that they sent women
to when they experienced a loss, and it only took a
couple of laps around the hallways to realize that I
wasn't the only one on the floor with a broken heart.
Our hospital used a yellow rose to mark the doors of
mothers who had experienced a loss, a quiet symbol
to remind all staff to speak gently and to not say
something insensitive. There was a rose on my
door...and another on a door around the corner from
me. For two days I worked up enough courage to
reach out to my neighbor by writing a brief note, just
to say, "I'm here, too. You aren't alone."

As it turned out, by the time I gave the note to a
nurse, the other mother had been discharged. But
that experience, within the first few days of my loss,

showed me three important things. First, I wasn't alone. Second, when I reached out to another hurting mom, taking a moment to look outward from my own hurt, my burden lifted just a bit as well. And third, no one understands a mother's broken heart than another mom who has walked that road. My path was set. I knew I had a long road of healing ahead of me, but I also knew it would include reaching out to others who had experienced the loss of a baby during pregnancy or early infancy. And in that place, the seeds were planted for what would become Naomi's Circle, a website with local and Internet-based information for baby loss parents, as well as a real-life support group for women at all stages on the loss journey, including recent loss, miscarriage, stillbirth, infant death, pregnancy after loss, and those who are now reaching out to others with their own ministries.

Perhaps you are thinking the same thing, that you would like your loss to mean something and for your experience to help others. If you are, here are some things to keep in mind.

Give yourself time. Soon after losing Naomi, I checked into the possibility of being trained to help other bereaved parents. I was disappointed to find that the organization I looked into wouldn't consider training me until I was 18 months out from my first loss. When I vented about this to my grief counselor, she gently agreed with them, pointing out that the generally accepted timeline is that it takes 18 to 24 months for bereaved parents to pass through (not "get over") the hardest part of the grieving process.

It is hard to support others when you are still struggling to survive yourself. This doesn't mean that you can't do anything to help others in the early days after your loss. However, if you are thinking about getting involved with any kind of one-on-one mentoring or beginning a support group, it is wise to take time to begin the healing process on your own before you start pouring into the lives of others.

Check your motives. Think carefully about why you want to reach out to others. Is your motive compassion? Wanting your child's life to make a difference? A realization of the needs of others? All of these are wonderful reasons. At times, however, my own desire to reach out to others has come from a less healthy place, such as wanting to stay busy, for example, to avoid a too-quiet home, and pouring my time and energy into reaching out to other hurting moms, but letting other relationships, like with my husband or living children, languish. Have an honest heart-to-heart with yourself from time to time to try to understand what is pushing you to spend your time the way you are.

Find a felt need. What need exists that you are drawn to meet? We found early into our loss journey that it was very hard to find information about local resources for bereaved parents. Resources were out there, but most were not advertised online or anywhere else. We decided that we would create a website where we could pull together all the loss information for our city into one place where parents could find it easily. We also knew that the only support groups in our city were at least a thirty-minute drive from where we lived, and we aspired to begin a group in our area to meet the needs of parents there. There are many websites, blogs, and organizations out there. Some provide support and information, while others offer financial assistance with burial costs, something soft to hold, photographs, and memorial items. Ask yourself, what need did you have in your time of loss that was not met adequately? Is that something you can help with now?

Determine your passions and your areas of giftedness. The flip side of need is to ask what *you* can do about it. What gifts and passions do you have? Are you a photographer? a writer? a seamstress? an advocate? Are you passionate about a particular cause, like SIDS or birth defects, or how hospitals and doctors deal with loss?

Along with meeting the need of parents to find local resources, Naomi's Circle is a vehicle for us to address one of our passions, reaching out to churches, mobilizing pastors and lay ministers to reach out to bereaved parents with compassion and understanding so that church, which is often a very painful place after a loss, can be the place of healing that it should be. My gifts are in the areas of writing, administration, and teaching, as well as showing mercy, and those are the areas where I work within our ministry.

Set realistic, yet lofty, goals. You don't want to set a goal so high that you will wither in discouragement when you don't meet it, but you also don't want to underestimate what you can do. Reaching out does not always mean establishing your own nonprofit or writing a blog that goes viral. It can be as simple as speaking with a coworker who has just had a miscarriage and letting her know she is not alone. Or buying a bouquet of yellow roses for your church's altar on Pregnancy and Infant Loss Awareness Sunday. If you would like to impact a larger audience, go for it! Find out what you can about blogging, writing, and how to interact with the media, or how to work with a bereavement photography service, like Now I Lay Me Down To Sleep.

Find ways to fill your own cup. Giving to others is exhausting, and if you are not filling your own emotional reserves, you will find yourself too empty to give any more. Think of it like those directions on a plane: put on your own oxygen mask before you help with someone else's. Make sure you are being filled emotionally, spiritually, and relationally. Take breaks to recharge, and watch for signs of burnout. Have a friend you can trust to ask you the hard questions, and be careful not to overcommit yourself or get involved in helping in ways that you are not equipped.

Keep your balance. There is more to life after loss than just loss. Take time for other things, such as family, fun, relaxation, and activities, that are apart from talking and thinking about babies who die too early. I am not saying this to be cold. You *need* those other outlets. You never forget, but you also need to have times that nurture your growth in other ways.

I remember the first time after Naomi's death when I found myself at an activity where other people didn't know about our loss and there was really no opportunity to tell anyone about her. A part of me was sad about that, but another part breathed a sigh of relief. For a short time, I could just be…me. I was still trying to figure out who that was post-loss, but I felt a sense of freedom to participate in something where I didn't have to focus on grief and death and being "that woman who lost a baby."

Four years after we started on the road of Pregnancy Loss, I am amazed at how God has used, and continues to use, the lives of my children in heaven to impact others. And more than amazed, I am grateful. While I will never know the "reason" I couldn't bring my babies home, helping others has shown me the purpose of their brief lives: to shower others on the same road with love and compassion, helping them move forward in their journey until they are strong enough to turn around to the person just beginning and reassure them, as I tried to in the hospital four years ago, "I'm here, too. You're not alone."

The TTTS Support Team

By Christina Russo-Sporer

December 15, 2010, was the day that my life changed forever. It was around 8:30 in the morning when an ultrasound technician rubbed the wand over my belly, once…twice…three times, then paused and said the words that no one wants to hear: "I can't find a heartbeat." Then she laid her head on my stomach.

When I look back on that day and the many hard ones that would follow, my heart is warmed by her show of emotion. This simple gesture was the first drop of water into a bucket that would soon overflow. The amount of love and support showed to me during this time in my life was so big that I will never be able to pay it back. I can only hope to pay it forward.

Twenty minutes later she was leading me out of the office building into the adjacent hospital. We headed towards the third floor of the Centennial building which housed the high-risk pregnancy ward. She introduced me to the RN on duty, who walked me into a large, empty hospital room.

I looked around the room. It was big, white, and empty, which is also a description for how I felt inside; lost and empty. I had nothing left to give; but as the day went on, both the room and my heart began to fill up with the colors of love and support.

I picked up my phone and began to deliver the news to my friends and family. I told them that Tyler was gone but Chase was alive and seemed to be healthy. At this point, we were not sure what was going to happen next. The perinatologist had to wait to consult with the neonatologist to form a plan.

The neonatologist explained to us that a fetus is viable outside the womb at 24 weeks, but the chances of survival are slim. The goal for me was to get to the 28-week mark and then re-evaluate. I would stay in the hospital and have 24-hour monitoring and a daily ultrasound.

Delivery at 28 weeks probably meant a surviving child, but it did not necessarily mean a healthy child. If born that early, Chase would be at risk for blindness, birth defects, and cerebral palsy.

As it already stood, we didn't know if Chase suffered any brain damage or illness from the passing of Tyler. There is always a chance that the twin who dies can bleed out into the surviving twin and cause brain damage.

The next two weeks seemed to drag on forever. I settled into a daily routine.

During these weeks, I learned who my true friends were. People who I never expected to come through came to visit me. They brought homemade meals and presents. Most importantly, they brought themselves. They gave of their time to care for me.

On the other hand, some people who I expected would be there for me every second were not. Their absence will be forever noticed.

About two days before New Year's Eve, I had passed our goal of 28 weeks, and Chase seemed to be faring well. The doctor let me go home for the remainder of the pregnancy, provided I went to the perinatologist office for daily ultrasounds and NST's (non-stress tests).

I'll never forget how good it felt to go home on that Thursday. The house smelled like a cinnamon candle, and the Christmas tree was still in good shape. My husband went shopping and filled the house with healthy foods. I was so glad to be able to sleep in my own bed.

My mom came up for New Year's, and I was tired and went to bed before midnight. I was awakened by the fireworks that our city sets off at midnight. I watched them through my bedroom window and cried and cried.

The ultrasounds continued to look good well into January. It wasn't until the last week of January in 2011 that Chase's cord blood flow numbers started to decrease every day. The first "bad" ultrasound occurred on a Thursday.

On Monday, I expressed my concerns to the doctor about the dangers of continuing the pregnancy. He agreed that it was time to end the pregnancy and that I would deliver that day.

Jason and I checked into the hospital late Monday afternoon. We tried to induce labor, but I would not dilate. Around 9 p.m. on Tuesday, Chase's oxygen levels started to fail, and I was brought in for an emergency C-section.

My twins were born around 10 p.m. on Tuesday, January 25th. Tyler was born sleeping, weighing 14 ounces and measuring 12 inches long. I got to spend some time with Tyler, but I was taken aback by the way he looked. I did not get a chance to hold him and say all that I wanted to say, and this is one of the biggest regrets of my life. We had him blessed by a pastor and chose to have him cremated. We did not have a funeral, which is another regret.

Chase was rushed to the NICU for the start of his four-week stay. He was born at 3 pounds 2 ounces, and continued to get bigger and stronger every day. He was finally released from the hospital on February 18, 2011, weighing less than 5 pounds. Thankfully he did not have any major neurological issues. He is one year behind developmentally but is expected to catch up.

Now that we were home, it was time to start the healing. I had been added to the TTTS Grief Support site on the day Tyler died, and I started to make many friends. Eventually another group opened called Survivors with Guardian Angels. I joined that one too. These are private groups. No one can see what you write besides the other members, so it is a safe place to vent. The women and men on the sites were amazing. They answered my questions, listened to my rants, and comforted me while I cried. I tried to give back to the other members of the group by offering the same support.

I was never the type of person to pour my heart out to total strangers, but just like sharing a religion, favorite sports team, or political affiliation, sharing a common tragedy brings people together. By the time Chase turned one, I had made many close online friends.

One night, several of us were chatting, and we were discussing the need to support women who were experiencing a new loss. I told them about my college friend, Tova Gold, who is also a contributor to this book. She was there for me from day one, first informing me, and then counseling me and sending me amazing care packages to the hospital.

We decided that we wanted to do something to help women who are experiencing a new loss, and I agreed to head up the team. This is how the T.T.S. Support Team was born. In the 1.5 years that we have been established (since December 2011), we have grown to 23 active package senders in the United States, Canada, Australia, and the United Kingdom. We also have received donated items to include in the packages, such as slipper socks, Teeny Tears diapers, and jewelry.

We have sent almost 100 packages, and they have gone out to every corner of the world. Each package is a labor of love and is funded by the package sender. They include items such as warm slipper socks, a picture frame for a sonogram picture, a journal, chocolate, candles, and a brochure with many resources for a woman who is suffering the loss of a stillborn or newborn child (this was designed by a loss mom and printed by another loss mom). We are continuing to grow, and there is a website coming in the near future. Working on this team is a way for us to help others but also keep alive the names and memories of our angels.

I have also had the privilege of meeting many of my "virtual" friends in person, and they are just as wonderful in real life as they are online. I text and call the ones who live too far away to meet, and they feel like old friends who I haven't seen in a while. One even feels like a long-lost sister.

In addition to my online friends, I was put in touch with a local woman by my perinatologist. She had just lost a twin and was looking to find someone to talk to. I called her on the phone, and we spoke for a long time. Since then we have formed a friendship, and our families have enjoyed many fun times together.

Losing Tyler broke me. There is not one day that I do not think of him, miss him, and wish he were in my arms. At the same time, I would not want to go back to being the person I was before his death. I have become a stronger person, a better Christian, and a more compassionate human being. Through the love and support of my family, friends, and healthcare workers, I found a voice that I didn't know I had.

First Peter 1:6 from the New Living Translation of the Bible reads, "So be truly glad, there is wonderful joy ahead even if it is necessary for you to endure many trials for a while."

If you are suffering a new loss, know that this tragedy has come into your life for a reason. You are now faced with a choice. You can succumb to the dark feelings and give up (which at times is a very tempting option), or you can choose to work through the pain and wait to see what blessings lie ahead.

Love,
Christina

Brie Bags

By Sarah Hackett

I am a thirty-four-year-old high-school anatomy teacher. I married my husband Paul on October 25, 2008, and we bought our first home the following spring. We bought a three-bedroom home with a bonus room and immediately made plans to start a family. Getting pregnant for the first time proved to be slightly difficult for us, but after trying for nine months, I was elated with a positive pregnancy test in April 2010. We were overjoyed!

From the beginning, my husband was sure the baby would be a boy, and we started organizing our spare bedroom in preparation for a nursery. My pregnancy was textbook. I passed every visit with flying colors. In July, we found out we were expecting a girl! I always dreamed of having a little girl, with her daddy's dark hair and my hazel eyes. As soon as we found out she was a girl, I started decorating the nursery. I painted canvas prints of scriptures, and we chose a name; I painted her monogram to hang on her wall. We had three baby showers, and our closets were overflowing with diapers, pink clothes, and toys. Our little girl, Brie (Brienna Katherine Hackett), was due on December 15, 2010. The funny thing was my sister was pregnant at the same time, and we shared the same due date!

She was expecting a boy, but it was still neat to compare pregnancy symptoms and talk about raising our children together.

My nephew Gabriel was born two weeks early on November 30th. I remember talking to Brie in my belly (as I did often) and telling her it was just the two of us for the next two weeks. But Brie didn't make it two more weeks. In the early morning hours of December 2, my husband and I went in the hospital with contractions that had kept me up for most of the night. I now know that those were very strong Braxton Hicks, but we believe it was God's way of getting us to the hospital before too much time had passed.

Being my first pregnancy, I expected to be sent home. We were escorted to the Maternal Assessment Center (MAC) unit to monitor my contractions. They put the monitor on me, as I got comfortable on the bed. I refused to have my husband call anyone (except my boss, since I was missing work) until we knew if we would need to stay. As we were whispering to each other about who to call when, I noticed that the technician just kept moving the monitor around.

"Is there a problem?" my husband asked.

She excused herself and said she needed to get the doctor. Our doctor came in and explained that sometimes the baby is in a strange position, and it's difficult to find her. I found that weird, since that had never happened to me. She tried the monitor, but to no avail. She called for an ultrasound — stat. I started shaking and started crying, "Where's my baby?" (The tears still flow, years later.)

When they brought the ultrasound machine in, our worst fears were confirmed. Somehow, little Brie had passed away. Time stopped. *Passed away? How is this possible? How could this be happening to me?* My mind was swirling in a million directions. I thought I would vomit, and then I had no energy to hold my head up. The tears started and continued. I'm not sure when they stopped.

They gave us two options: either induce immediately, or go home, process the information, and come back later to induce. Either way, I was going to have to go through labor and delivery and deliver my dead baby. I was never going to bring her home. She would never cry. *Oh, God...how is this happening to us?!* We chose to induce immediately and began a round of Cytotec. We didn't start the Pitocin until the next morning.

Brienna Katherine Hackett was born at 3:30 p.m. on December 3, 2010, weighing 5 pounds 10 ounces and measuring 21 inches long. She had her daddy's dark hair and my hazel eyes, just like I always imagined. We held her for hours. We dressed her. The "Now I Lay Me Down to Sleep" volunteer photographer came and took beautiful pictures of her that we cherish. The nursing staff got beautiful impressions of her hands and feet. I will always treasure the little time we had with our sweet firstborn baby girl. Some parents never know what caused the passing of their full-term baby. I'm not sure if it's better to know or not. Sometimes too much information causes more anxiety. For us, that was the case.

After she was born, we found out that her umbilical cord hadn't developed perfectly at the attachment place, which had caused it to twist. The cause of death was torsion of the umbilical cord. The chances of it happening are slim to none. It is so rare that it cannot be detected by ultrasound; the baby develops correctly, adapts, and simply passes away toward the end of the pregnancy. There is no cause. There is no prevention. There was nothing we could have done. There was no way for us to have known. It is simply a medical anomaly. It could happen in subsequent pregnancies, but it probably won't. With all of our medical advances today, we really have no idea what causes this or any way to prevent it.

We had a little service for her a few days later. It was impromptu, and only a few family members and close friends were able to come. We didn't pick out her grave marker or cemetery plot until a month later. Her true funeral was two months later, when I was emotionally ready to make the decisions we were too blindsided for then. Some people didn't understand why we postponed her service. We chose to cremate her remains, so it was really a decision we could wait to make. My husband and I realize that with loss, many people don't understand a lot of things about it. We gave up trying to answer everyone's questions. I didn't touch our nursery. It stayed the exact same for six months.

There isn't a day that goes by where I don't miss her. I wonder what she would have been like and who my husband and I would be today if she had lived. We are still ourselves, but we are *different* versions of ourselves. There was the Sarah and PJ before Brie, and there is the Sarah and PJ after Brie. I know many couples make different decisions following the loss of a full-term baby. We decided to go to grief counseling and support groups, which empowered us to survive and keep going. Some couples decide not to have any other children; some even have to face infertility following a loss like ours. We chose to trust God, and we believed we would be parents one day. But those first few hours, days, weeks, and months were horrible. The devastations, depression, and sadness in our home were palpable. We both returned to work, but we were shadows of our previous selves. It took us a long time to try to get back to "normal." Even today, three years later, there are days when it all comes back. But it gets easier. Time helps.

The doctor told us it would be safe to get pregnant again within a few months. I was prescribed antianxiety medication, so I gave my body time to wean off of those before we entertained the idea of getting pregnant again. *What if it happened again? Could we survive another loss?* I told my husband that if we had another loss, I was done getting pregnant. I don't think he believed me. We were pregnant again within six months.

There are a lot of misconceptions with losing a baby. People think that after a few weeks, you're simply over it. *You are* never *over it.* They think that once you get pregnant again, the baby who was lost is forgotten. Some people even thought we got pregnant again to *replace* Brie. We could never replace her! Being pregnant again was emotionally draining. Every day I was afraid I would lose the baby again.

Most people worry about having a miscarriage before the end of the first trimester; I worry about losing the baby at the end. People would stop me in the grocery store and congratulate me on my first pregnancy; sometimes I would correct them (if I was feeling strong), and some days I would just smile and nod. Sometimes it's just not a complete stranger's business to hear my story...and yet sometimes it is.

Since Brie's condition couldn't be detected by ultrasound, we really couldn't do much differently during my second pregnancy, except to pray and trust that this time things would end differently. For my last month, my doctors categorized me as "highly monitored," and I basically lived at my OB's office, sitting on the monitor for twenty minutes a day and having weekly ultrasounds. The MAC unit became my home away from home. They kept reminding me that they wouldn't be able to see if our second child had the same issue, but they could monitor the heartbeat and activity level and know if he/she slowed down. The extra monitoring put a strain on our bank account but I slept at night.

The minute Isabel Janice Hackett was born on January 28, 2012, I feel that my husband and I breathed for the first time since losing Brie. Everything about her birth was different. I had never given birth to a baby who cried; I had never breastfed my child. I had never brought a baby home. We had never used the nursery.

Isabel is now nineteen months old. She has fulfilled so many of our needs; she has filled our home with laughter and her incredible energy. Her name means "chosen and consecrated to God," and it could not be more perfectly suited to her. She is indeed our "rainbow baby," the baby that comes after loss, reminiscent of the rainbow God brought to Noah after the devastating flood.

Today Brie has a legacy. With the help of my support group, I have started Mommy to Mommy Outreach, an organization that provides "Brie Bags" to the labor and delivery floors for families dealing with a late miscarriage or stillborn. Each bag is sewn by me or other volunteers, mostly mothers of loss. We provide a cap and diaper for the baby, a book on dealing with loss, a bookmark, and an angel teddy bear. We also provide links to support groups in the area. We have heard from some ladies who tell us that the bags were such a blessing to their family. We may not ever get feedback from some ladies, so the few we do have contact with makes it worth it.

I feel it's my job to help other families now dealing with their loss. We can't stop loss from happening, but we can make it easier on families to deal with it. In the last four months, over fifty bags have been delivered to area hospitals or mailed to individual families. That's fifty families that will know they are not alone in their grief. They are not alone in their loss. They will survive.

For more information, feel free to contact me at mommytomommy29073@gmail.com or visit our support group's website at www.naomiscircle.org, and follow the M2M tab for more information on getting involved in Mommy to Mommy Outreach.

Sincerely,
Sarah

The Henry Michael Powell Memorial Garden for Children

By Kelly Powell

When we lost Henry seven years ago, it was important to us to build a place of joy to help us remember the joy he brought us. A children's garden establishes a creative space for education, learning, creativity, play, and, in the quieter moments, reflection. We decided we wanted Henry's future siblings to have a place to visit that was established because of their brother, and to know his life has contributed to a beautiful spot we hope will be filled with laughter and learning. We look forward to the day we can bring his sisters Annalise and Isabel to "his" garden and they can share their brother's legacy with their friends. Along with the memorial aspect of the project, we also hope this special place creates new memories for children who visit it. The Hampton-Preston Garden Restoration Project is a historically-inspired design which will reflect the antebellum period of the property.

The first phase of the project began in the fall of 2011 and includes a Welcome Garden, Fountain Garden, and Children's Garden including Henry's memorial space. The Children's Garden will be a walled garden designed to a child's scale. This garden will surround a new antebellum-style gazebo and memorial space, and will appeal to a child's sense of exploration and discovery, including spaces to foster active, creative, and imaginative play. In a larger sense, we hope the historically accurate setting will help identify and communicate to visitors of all ages a sense of the interconnectedness of all the generations through fundamentally common experience, which will enhance our common perspective not just of the past, but also the present and the future. We could not think of a better way for Henry's short life to positively imprint the lives of others than to dedicate the memorial funds that our friends and family contributed in Henry's memory to this project.

I have become more resilient and have gained an incredible perspective on what is important, what is difficult, and what is impossible. I read Elizabeth Edwards's book, *Saving Graces*, shortly after Henry died. She lost her sixteen-year-old son in a car accident in 1996. She wrote of the "strange gift" of his death: "I had the gift of knowing that nothing will ever be as bad as that. The worst day of my life had already come." This observation has stuck with me and helped me know that nothing that can happen to me, short of losing my two daughters, can ever be as difficult.

Blessings,
Kelly

Child Dancing, Heart's Delight

Child dancing, heart's delight
Petals floating, happy light.
Angels waiting, face benign,
"This small child is one of mine."

Fragrant blossoms, fresh with dew,
Princely garland over you.
Tinkling music, a fairy's laugh
Leads the frolic down the path.

Mighty fortress sound, secure,
to shelter children coming here.
Wooden doors lead to the hall;
I know this one! I know them all!

Happy voices, "Come and eat!"
For you, there's always been a seat.
A room, a hearth, a forever be
With forever views on acorn trees.

Calmly playing, heart content,
waiting till my family's sent.
Bright eyes twinkling — King divine!
"This small child is one of mine."

— Jennie Goutet

Conclusion - You Are Not Alone

As you have read this book, we hope that you have made some connections and found some encouragement.

This is not an easy road, but you do not have to walk it alone.

You will find all of our contact information in the Contributors Bios section at the end of the book. If you want to reach out to any of us, we are here for you.

Please visit our website at **http://sunshineafterstorm.us**

FaceBook **http://www.facebook.com/SunshineAftertheStorm**

If you found this book helpful or meaningful, we would appreciate positive reviews on Amazon and GoodReads.

From my heart to yours,

Alexa Bigwarfe
President and Founder
Sunshine After the Storm, Inc.

Grief Checklist

This is a tool to help you build a list to help others help you.

Friends and family may ask to help, but they may not have any idea of what would be helpful to you. It is wonderful when people just DO things, but often they may ask you what you need. It's so hard to answer that question, so we're here to help.

This may look familiar, because Suzanne Tucker created this list for her contribution to the book.

You can use this as a template, modify it to what makes you feel comfortable or would help you, add to it, remove the things you don't like, and then give it to people when they ask how they can help.

My Grief To-Do List

- Listen. Just listen and allow for my grief. This is the most powerful thing you can do.

- Tell me you are sorry.

- Tell me you are thinking of me.

- Tell me you are praying for me, and then do, every night if you can.

- Send me something small to remind me how much you care or simply call to see how I am doing.

- Hug me. Even when I tell you I'm okay, hug me anyway.

- Say my baby's name. I love to hear it.

- Put this date on your calendar:

_____

and remember my angel with me, year after year.

- Make me laugh. Laughter is often the best medicine.

- Give me the gift of you. Your heart. Your tears. Your understanding. Your love. Your permission to grieve.

Grief Resources

There are many, many resources for grieving parents, whether you are looking for books or blogs to read, tokens of remembrance, or communities. The following is a list of some of our favorite sites and resources. It is certainly not inclusive, and we welcome your input and additions to these resources on our Facebook page (http://www.facebook.com/sunshineafterthestorm) and our website (http://sunshineafterstorm.us).

If you are interested in finding the websites, Facebook pages, and other social media accounts for the contributors in this book, please go to the Contributor Bios section.

Books
Empty Arms by Sherokee Ilse
Forever Linked: A Mother's Journey through Twin to Twin Transfusion Syndrome by Erin Bruch
Grieving Dads: To the Brink and Back by Kelly Farley
I Will Carry You: The Sacred Dance of Grief and Joy by Angie Smith
Toughest Teeniest Twin Soldiers by Wendy R. Smith

Baby Loss and Grief Websites

A Place to Remember (bookstore, gift items)
http://www.aplacetoremember.com/
Babies Remembered:
http://www.BabiesRemembered.org
Baby Angel Pics (photo retouching)
http://www.babyangelpics.com/

Bereaved Parents of the USA
http://www.bereavedparentsusa.org/
Bereavement Store
http://bereavementstore.com/
Casting Keepsakes
http://www.castingkeepsakes.com/
Christian's Beach (names written in the sand)
http://namesinthesand.blogspot.com/
CLIMB (Center for Loss in Multiple Births)
http://www.climb-support.org/
Compassionate Friends (support for loss)
http://www.compassionatefriends.org/home.aspx
Faces of Loss Faces of Hope (local support)
http://facesofloss.com/
Finding My Muchness - Finding Light after loss
http://findingmymuchness.com
Fight TTTS – Information/Awareness
http://fightTTTS.com
Grief Song (grief songs)
http://www.griefsong.com/
Halo Garden
http://www.halogarden.com/
Hannah's Prayer
http://www.hannah.org
Healing Hearts (information)
http://www.babylosscomfort.com/grief-resources/
Heartbreaking Choice (For parents who have terminated due to poor prenatal diagnosis)
http://www.aheartbreakingchoice.com/
In the Face of Loss (on making time and space for grief)
http://Www.inthefaceofloss.com
In the Name of the Fire (grief website)
http://inthenameofthefire.wordpress.com/
Little Angels Online Store
http://www.littleangelsonlinestore.com/Store/
Living with Loss Magazine
http://www.livingwithloss.com/page.cfm?pageid=9009

Loss Doulas International
http://www.LossDoulasInternational.com
Memory Of (memorial website)
http://www.memory-of.com/Public/
MEND
http://www.mend.org
Mikayla's Grace (provides care packages to grieving parents, WI)
http://www.mikaylasgrace.com
Molly Bears (bear created in the same weight as your baby)
http://www.mollybears.com/
Mommies with Hope
http://www.mommieswithhope.com
My Forever Child (keepsakes and jewelry)
http://www.myforeverchild.com/
Nechamama Comfort (Jewish pregnancy and loss support program)
http://www.nechamacomfort.org
Now I Lay Me Down To Sleep (photography)
http://www.nowilaymedowntosleep.org/
No Holding Back (blog on life after loss)
http://katbiggie.com
October 15th (pregnancy and infant loss awareness)
http://www.october15th.com/
Perfect Joy Ministries
http://www.perfectjoyministries.com
Pencil Portraits by Dana
http://portraitsbydana.com/
Piggie Paws (creates handprints/footprints into something else)
http://www.piggiesandpaws.com/
Project Heal (and International Bereaved Mother's Day)
http://carlymarieprojectheal.com/
Rainbows and Redemption: Encouragement for the Journey of Pregnancy After Loss
http://www.rainbowsandredemption.weebly.com
Remembering Our Babies (memorial keepsakes and jewelry)
http://www.rememberingourbabies.net/
Return to Zero
http://returntozerothemovie.com/
SHARE (pregnancy/infant loss support groups)

http://www.nationalshare.org/
SPALS (pregnancy after loss)
http://www.spals.com/home/index.html
Stillborn Memorial (pencil sketches)
http://www.stillbornmemorial.com
Still Standing Magazine (surviving child loss and infertility)
http://stillstandingmag.com
Sufficient Grace Ministries
http://www.sufficientgraceministries.org
Teeny Tears (diapers for micro and super micro preemies)
http://www.teenytears.blogspot.com
The Greatest Blessing (memory boxes)
http://www.greatestblessing.blogspot.com/
TTTS Support Team (care packages for parents who have lost one or both twins to TTTS)
http://www.tttsgriefsupport.com
Virtual Memorials (create remembrance site)
http://www.virtual-memorials.com/

Facebook

Fetal Hope Foundation
http://www.facebook.com/pages/Fetal-Hope-Foundation/70302707927

March of Dimes
https://www.facebook.com/marchofdimes

Sunshine After the Storm
http://www.facebook.com/SunshineAftertheStorm

The Invisible Mom's Club
https://www.facebook.com/groups/235156183298999/

Transcending Loss: Understanding the Lifelong Impact of Grief
https://www.facebook.com/transcendingloss

TTTS Foundation
http://www.facebook.com/groups/tttsfoundation/

Contributor Bios

Alexa Bigwarfe

Alexa is the mother of four beautiful children, three on earth and one in heaven. She is a freelance writer and also blogs at *No Holding Back – Life after the Loss*, primarily focused on finding joy after grief of the loss of one of her twins, but also about raising three small children as a stay-at-home mom. A major focus is also on bringing more awareness to TTTS, and providing hope to other grieving mothers. Find her at: http://katbiggie.com, http://fightTTTS.com; www.facebook.com/NoHoldingBack1212; and http://www.twitter.com/katbiggie.

Amy Hillis

Amy is a mother to seven, five here on earth and two in heaven. Three of her children have had liver transplants, and she is a fierce advocate for organ donation. She currently resides with her three youngest boys in a small town just outside of Cincinnati, OH. Find her at: http://transplantedx3.wordpress.com; https://www.facebook.com/TransplantedThoughts; and https://www.twitter.com/transplantedx3.

Anna Whiston-Donaldson

Anna is a former high-school English teacher and a writer. Anna lost her twelve-year-old son in a neighborhood accident. She blogs about life and the loss of Jack at the blog *An Inch of Gray*. Her memoir will be published in September 2014 by Convergent Books, a division of Random House. Find her at: http://www.aninchofgray.blogspot.com;

https://www.facebook.com/aninchofgray; and
https://www.twitter.com/aninchofgray.

AnnMarie Cameron Gubenko

AnnMarie is a former teacher, aspiring writer, and stay-at-home mom of four here on earth and one in heaven. She married her college sweetheart, and together they are riding this roller coaster of life. When not shuffling kids to football, basketball, baseball, cheerleading, volleyball, and ballet, and folding and putting away the endless mounds of laundry that a family of six creates, she loves to read, write, and can often be found at Target or Barnes & Noble. She is the author of *Tidbits from the Queen of Chaos*, which is a blog about the ups and downs of marriage to a sports-loving extrovert, and motherhood involving a teen, twin tweens, and a preschooler. Topics such as infertility, life with children that battle a chronic illness, and triumphing through tragedy are also covered. It's not always pretty, but it's always honest. Find her at: http://tidbitsqueenchaos.com/; https://www.facebook.com/tidbitsfromthequeenofchaos; and https://twitter.com/queenofchaosmom.

Christina Russo-Sporer

Christina was raised in rural Pennsylvania and attended college in New York City. She loves bumming around NYC, traveling to the Caribbean, drinking good microbrews, and eating ice cream. The loss of her son Tyler in 2010 changed her main focus in life from her fashion career to helping women who are suffering through the loss of a child. She currently lives in Bethlehem, PA, with her husband Jason, son Chase, and Boston terrier Fizz. She runs the TTTS (Twin to Twin Transfusion Syndrome) Support Team to provide care packages to mothers who have recently lost one or both twins to TTTS, found at http://www.tttsgriefsupport.com Contact her at: **Chrissporer1122@gmail.com**.

Dana Loewenstein Weinstein

Dana has over seventeen years' experience in direct response marketing, fourteen of which are concentrated in nonprofit fundraising and advocacy efforts. She has raised a hundreds of millions of dollars for organizations such as AARP, the Democratic National Committee, the United States Holocaust Memorial Museum, World Jewish Congress, and Hillel: The Foundation for Jewish Campus Life through multichannel fundraising. In July of 2009, Dana's world was turned upside down when at 31 weeks into her second pregnancy she received a shocking and devastating diagnosis—her unborn daughter's brain had several severe anomalies, resulting in a prognosis that was incompatible with life. Faced with the choice of carrying her baby to term, only to watch her seize to death upon deliver, or terminate her much-wanted pregnancy, Dana made the heartbreaking decision to end the pregnancy. She is vocal about her experience and feels passionately about helping the pro-choice movement in its efforts to preserve abortion rights through volunteering with NARAL and NAF. Dana is also committed to creating a world where open, honest, and emotional conversations about abortion experiences can occur.

Dana holds a master's degree from George Washington University and currently serves as the Director of Membership at the United States Holocaust Museum in Washington, DC. She has been happily married for nearly ten years and is mom to six-year old Nate, two-and-a-half-year-old Danica, and nine-week-old Isabella.

Heather O'Brien Webb

Heather O'Brien Webb is the married mother of two tween girls and a stillborn baby girl (July 1, 2012). She has been blogging since 2001 at *The Destiny Manifest,* where she writes about her family, coping with the full-term stillbirth of her youngest daughter, and appreciating the beautiful things that surround us. Every day is an adventure! Find her at: http://www.thedestinymanifest.com;

http://www.facebook.com/TheDestinyManifest; and
http://www.twitter.com/eatherhaelo.

Jennie Goutet

Jennie lives just outside of Paris and is the wife of a Frenchman, and mother to three of his children. Her work has appeared in *The Huffington Post,* Queen Latifah's website, *World Moms Blog,* and the *BlogHer* website. She was also honored twice as BlogHer Voice of the Year. Jennie blogs at *A Lady in France* about family, food, France, and faith. Her book *A Lady in France – A Memoir* is about her path to find God in face of grief, depression, and living abroad, is available for order on Amazon.com. Find her at: http://www.aladyinfrance.com; https://www.facebook.com/aladyinfrance; and http://www.twitter.com/aladyinfrance.

Jessica Watson

Jessica is a mom to five, four in her arms and one in her heart. After the loss of her daughter, one of triplets, in 2007, Jessica left the corporate world behind, vowed to soak up every living moment, and discovered her writing roots again. Her writing has been published at places such as *The Huffington Post,* SheKnows.com, *Still Standing Magazine,* and *Mamalode Magazine.* You can find her wearing her heart on her sleeve at her personal blog, *Four Plus an Angel.* Find her at:
http://www.fourplusanangel.com;
http://www.facebook.com/fourplusanangel; and
http://www.twitter.com/jessbwatson.

Kathy Radigan

Kathy R. is a writer, blogger, social media addict, mom to three, wife to one, and owner of a possessed kitchen appliance. She posts a weekly essay each Sunday on her blog, *My Dishwasher's Possessed,* which she started in the fall of 2010 when

her youngest child started kindergarten. Kathy also co-founded the online magazine *Bonbon Break* (www.bonbonbreak.com). She lives just outside New York City with her family and still finds it hysterical that the woman who didn't even have an e-mail address three years ago is now immersed in the online world. Find her at:
http://mydishwasherspossessed.blogspot.com;
http://www.facebook.com/Kathy.Radigan; and at
http://www.twitter.com/KathyRadigan.

Kathy Glow

Kathy G. is a freelance writer, blogger, and mother of five energetic boys living in Nebraska. When she is not driving all over town in her minivan, wiping "boy stuff" off the walls, or trying to find the bottom of the pile of laundry, she is writing about what life is really like after all your dreams come true on her blog, *Kissing the Frog*. Infertility, depression, grief, and the loss of her oldest son from cancer are some of things she never expected to find in her fairy-tale happy ending. A 2013 BlogHer Voices of the Year honoree, her writing has been featured on *Huffington Post Parents, Mamalode,* and *Mamapedia*. She is also a feature writer for Nebraska's online women's magazine, *Her View from Home*. Find her at: http://www.lifewiththefrog.com; https://www.facebook.com/pages/kissing-the-frog/155770194533025; and
https://twitter.com/lifewiththefrog.

Katia Bishops

Katia is a mother of two boys, a four-year-old and one-year-old. She writes about them and occasionally about her husband, thirty-seven years old. Currently on mat leave, she's fulfilling a lifelong dream to write and make people laugh. And sometimes cry, which was not her dream or intention. The serious stuff Katia writes about includes immigration, fertility, and miscarriage. Find her at: http://iamthemilk.wordpress.com and http://www.twitter.com/KatiaDBE. She also contributes regularly at http://www.mamapop.com.

Kelly DeBie

Kelly is a California girl living a Colorado life. She is lucky to be the mother of four amazing children and one angel baby. She is in the process of writing three books. She might moonlight as Wonder Woman, but no one can really be sure; they've never been seen in the same room. If you're not nice, she'll write about you. Find her at:
http://debiehive.blogspot.com;
https://www.facebook.com/debie.hive; and
https://twitter.com/DeBieHive.

Kelly Powell

Kelly is the proud mommy of Henry Michael (September 27, 2006–October 3, 2006), Annalise, and Isabel. Although Henry does not live with them on earth, he is forever in their hearts. To honor Henry, Kelly and her husband Keith established the Henry Michael Powell Memorial Garden, a beautiful children's garden in the historic district of Columbia, SC. Find her at:
https://www.facebook.com/HMPGarden.

Kristi Bothur

Growing up as an Air Force brat, Kristi Bothur claims anyplace she lives more than six months as "home." Kristi spent her twenties traveling the globe as she taught English as a Second Language both in the United States and internationally. She finally settled down in South Carolina, where she attended seminary at Columbia International University and met the love of her life, her husband Eric. The first decade of their marriage was filled with the joys of ministry, the conflict of "unexplained infertility," the thrill of becoming parents, the agony of losing three children in pregnancy, and the roller-coaster ride of the

journey of pregnancy after loss. Kristi is now a pastor's wife, a stay-at-home homeschooling mom to her two living children, and the founder of Naomi's Circle, a ministry to parents who have experienced the loss of a baby during pregnancy or early infancy. She is also a contributing editor to the e-devotional, *Rainbows and Redemption: Encouragement for the Journey of Pregnancy after Loss.* Find her at:
http://www.thissideofheaven.weebly.com;
http://www.naomisicircle.org; and
http://www.rainbowsandredemption.weebly.com.

Lizzi Rogers

Lizzi, blogs at *Considerings*, where she is trying to write her way through two early losses and subsequent diagnosis of spousal infertility. She hopes and strives to write the truth, the whole truth, and sometimes even something uplifting. And whilst she wishes no one had to go through the journey of child loss, she aims to contribute usefully to existing resources available to help those who are in that position. Find her at: http://summat2thinkon.blogspot.co.uk and "The Invisible Moms Club" Facebook page,
https://www.facebook.com/groups/235156183298999/.

Marcia Kester Doyle

Marcia is a native Floridian, married and the mother of four children and one grandchild. She is the author of the humorous blog *Menopausal Mother*, where she muses on the good, the bad, and the ugly side of menopausal mayhem. Marcia's work has appeared on *Scary Mommy, In the Powder Room, The Erma Bombeck Writers Workshop, Generation Fabulous, Mamapedia, Bloggy Moms, Messy Moms Radio, The Woven Tale Press*, and the *Life Well Blogged* series, and was voted top 25 in the Circle of Moms Contest 2013. Find her at:
http://www.menopausalmom.com;
http://www.facebook.com/MenopausalMother; and
http://www.twitter.com/MenoMother.

Rachel B. Raper

Rachel, speech language pathologist and owner of a private practice, is a wife and mother of two. Rachel began a ministry, Embracing Evan, in 2013 following her son's stillbirth the previous year. Rachel enjoys writing for therapeutic reasons and shares in attempts to support others through their grief.

Regina Petsch

Regina has been: a teenaged bride; a pregnant teenager; a divorcée; a single mother; a nontraditional college student; and remarried. She has been diagnosed with secondary infertility and is a woman who prayed, wished, and hoped for two blue lines on a pregnancy test, for more than six years, attempting so many different tactics to achieve pregnancy that to this day it boggles her mind. She is a woman who would seek the advice of infertility specialists, undergo three surgeries and every test imaginable, and begin a series of medications to attempt to get pregnant. She is a woman who would *finally* succeed at achieving pregnancy, only to miscarry in the first trimester, *twice*; she would try artificial insemination four months in a row, with *zero* success. Regina would choose in vitro fertilization in a last (and most expensive) attempt to have a baby, achieving what every "infertile" woman wants: a successful pregnancy that results in the near full-term delivery of a healthy son. She would achieve pregnancy through the miracle of IVF two more times and delivered two beautiful, tiny, and *very* premature babies — only one of which is alive today. She is a woman who would be crushed to the point of suicidal ideation, feeling as if she were literally drowning in grief, but would find a way to crawl out of a deep, dark, cavernous pit of despair — or be drowned in it. She would become the mother of a child who came home from the hospital via the morgue and a funeral home. Part of her healing journey has been to start blogging, where she has found a virtual support system like no other. It is through them that part of her story is included in this book. She writes, she still cries, and she mothers all five of her children to the best of her ability. She is human, and she will never again be completely whole until she is reunited with her son. Find her at: http://theapocalypticgingerchronicles.blogspot.com/ and https://www.facebook.com/TheApocalypticGingerChronicles.

Sandi Wright Haustein

Sandi is a freelance writer and a mom to three boys. Her fourth and fifth pregnancies ended in miscarriage. Find her at: https://www.facebook.com/sandihausteinwriter and https://twitter.com/sandihaus.

Sarah Hackett

Sarah is a thirty-three-year-old mother of two daughters, her oldest Brie, who would be three this December, and her youngest Isabel, who is twenty months old. She is expecting her third child in the spring. She is a high school anatomy teacher and resides in Lexington, SC, with her husband PJ. She started Mommy to Mommy Outreach, providing Brie Bags in honor of her oldest daughter to area hospitals. She works with Rachel Raper, sewing and providing 15 bags and Embracing Evan bears each month. For more information, feel free to e-mail her at mommytomommy29073@gmail.com.

Sarah Rudell Beach

Sarah is a teacher, wife, and mother to two little ones. She is the creator of *Left Brain Buddha*, where she explores ideas and practices for mindfulness, and shares the challenges and riches in her journey to live and parent mindfully in a left-brain, analytical life. She encourages us to discover the amazing transformations that can occur when we not only indulge, but learn to tame, our monkey minds. In her free time, she enjoys reading, yoga, and hanging out with her little Buddhas. Find her at: http://leftbrainbuddha.com;

http://facebook.com/leftbrainbuddha; and
http://www.twitter.com/LeftBrainBuddha.

Sheila Quirke

Sheila worked as a clinical social worker (focused on aging, bereavement counseling, and hospice) for ten years before her daughter was diagnosed with an aggressive brain tumor. After 31 months of treatment, her four-year-old daughter, Donna, died in 2009. When she returned to professional work in 2011, Sheila started a mom blog, the popular *Mary Tyler Mom,* to focus on parenting and working. Soon, though, Sheila came out of the closet as a grieving mom. In September 2011, to honor Childhood Cancer Awareness Month, Sheila wrote about her daughter's cancer treatment in serial format. "Donna's Cancer Story" was very well received and ran in *The Huffington Post* in September 2012. Using her social media presence as a platform, Sheila works to raise awareness and advocates for children with cancer and their families. No longer working in social work, Sheila now writes freelance articles in addition to her blog, as well as acting as executive director of Donna's Good Things, the charity created to honor her daughter and do good things in her name. Sheila lives in Chicago with her husband and son and has recently adopted a baby boy. She works hard to choose hope every day.

Find her at:

Donna's Good Things: http://www.donnasgoodthings.org and https://www.facebook.com/donnasgoodthings

Mary Tyler Mom: http://www.chicagonow.com/mary-tyler-mom;

https://www.facebook.com/pages/Mary-Tyler-Mom/159776680754263; and

https://twitter.com/MaryTylerMom

Starr Bryson

Starr works from her home in Arizona as a freelance writer. Her writing ranges from humor laced snark-fests and gritty and painfully raw nonfiction, all the way to her recently discovered

dark world of erotica. ("It pays the bills!" she proclaims.) The author behind *The Insomniac's Dream,* she claims blogging was only the beginning of an amazing freelancing career. She also writes fiction and is working on a book in her spare time, around all of her other deadlines and in between raising two fantastically funny and disgusting tween boys. Starr loves Halloween, zombies, and all things horror. She aspires to be a vampire someday. She enjoys adult grape juice, reading in her nonexistent spare time, and connecting with other writers, bloggers, and her readers. Her claim to fame is her caustic wit, copious swears, and an ongoing battle with insomnia. Happy Nightmares! Find her at:
http://www.theinsomniacsdream.com;
https://www.facebook.com/sleepybard; and
https://twitter.com/sleepybard.

Stephanie Sprenger

Stephanie is a music therapist, freelance writer, and mother of two girls, ages seven and two. She blogs at *Mommy, for Real* about the imperfect reality of surviving the daily grind with young kids, and *The HerStories Project* about women's friendship. Writing is her outlet for coping with chaos and the challenges of parenthood, and she tries to find time for yoga, meditation, reading, and enjoying wine or coffee with close friends whenever possible. Find her at:
http://www.stephaniesprenger.com;
http://www.herstoriesproject.com;
http://www.facebook.com/mommyforreal; and
http://www.twitter.com/mommyisforreal.

Suzanne M. Tucker

Suzanne is mom to nine, twins plus two and five angel babes. She created the *My Mommy Manual* website and community to encourage parents to look inside themselves for instructions, inspiration, and guidance. She leads weekly classes for new parents as a PT and infant massage educator in St.

Louis, Missouri, where she runs a holistic rehabilitation center with her business and life partner Shawn. Suzanne is the author of *In The Face Of Loss: A Companion Journal,* to be published in May of 2014. Find her at: http://MyMommyManual.com; http://InTheFaceOfLoss.com; http://www.facebook.com/MyMommyManual; http://www.facebook.com/InTheFaceOfLoss (page unpublished until 01/01/2014); and http://www.twitter.com/ZenMommy.

Tova Gold

Tova is the founder of FindingMyMuchness.com. Founded in memory of her twin daughters, forever nicknamed Sunshine and Daisy, who were stolen by TTTS in September 2009. *Finding My Muchness* is dedicated to helping women re-find their joy and identity after grief or trauma. Find her at: http://findingmymuchness.com; https://www.facebook.com/FindingMyMuchness; and https://twitter.com/FindingMuchness.

Wendy R. Smith

Wendy resides in Southern Nevada with her husband and two sons. She earned her English degree from the University of Nevada Las Vegas and works as a data analyst in healthcare. She loves spending time with her family, and enjoys reading and writing and practically any outdoor activity, be it mountains or the lake. It has become Wendy's personal mission to spread the word about Twin to Twin Transfusion Syndrome (TTTS) and to remind all baby-loss mothers that they are not alone in their journey. She is also involved in a local bereavement support group, Healing Hearts Giving Hope! Find her at:

Http://facebook.com/TTTSToughestTeeniestTwinSoldiers

Made in the USA
Columbia, SC
30 May 2023

17524053R00192